NEW ZEALAND'S
TOP FRANCHISE
LEADERS

T0362962

GLOBAL
PUBLISHING
G R O U P

Global Publishing Group
Australia • New Zealand • Singapore • America • London

NEW ZEALAND'S TOP FRANCHISE LEADERS

INTERNATIONAL NO. 1 BEST SELLER

SECRETS REVEALED

How to Build Wealth & Success in Franchising

PETE BURDON

International Author, Branding Expert and Media Trainer

DISCLAIMER

All the information, techniques, skills and concepts contained within this publication are of the nature of general comment only and are not in any way recommended as individual advice. The intent is to offer a variety of information to provide a wider range of choices now and in the future, recognising that we all have widely diverse circumstances and viewpoints. Should any reader choose to make use of the information contained herein, this is their decision, and the contributors (and their companies), authors and publishers do not assume any responsibilities whatsoever under any condition or circumstances. It is recommended that the reader obtain their own independent advice.

First Edition 2020

Copyright © 2020 Pete Burdon

All rights are reserved. The material contained within this book is protected by copyright law, no part may be copied, reproduced, presented, stored, communicated or transmitted in any form by any means without prior written permission.

National Library of Australia
Cataloguing-in-Publication entry:

New Zealand's Top Franchise Leaders, Secrets Revealed. How to Build Wealth & Success in Franchising. - Pete Burdon

1st ed.
ISBN: 978-1-925370-00-3 (pbk.)

 A catalogue record for this book is available from the National Library of Australia

Published by Global Publishing Group
PO Box 517 Mt Evelyn, Victoria 3796 Australia
Email Info@GlobalPublishingGroup.com.au

Printed in Australia

For further information about orders:
Phone: +61 3 9726 4133

*I dedicate this book to franchisors
and other business owners who
put everything on the line to create
companies that benefit so many other
people, whether they be franchisees or
employees. Without these courageous
risk-takers, our standard of living
would take a serious nosedive.*

ACKNOWLEDGMENTS

Writing this book has been an amazing journey from the minute the idea was sparked. As with any project like this, it couldn't have been done without the help of so many people.

At the top of that list is Darren Stephens. Darren has written many similar bestsellers and the support and advice he's given me throughout the process has been priceless. The business mastermind group run by Darren and wife Jackie in Melbourne, 'The Entrepreneurs Inner Circle', has been the catalyst for making the book not only possible, but a bestseller.

The next group to thank are the Top New Zealand Franchise Leaders featured in the book. It's been a privilege to get to know them and hear their stories. What stood out for me with every one of them was their total commitment to their franchisees. You'll see this for yourself in the following pages along with other reasons why they are so successful.

Simon Lord also deserves a special mention. He is one of New Zealand's most respected franchise experts and his Foreword and 'Next Steps' chapter really add value to the book.

Last, but certainly not least, I thank my wife Steph and daughter Olivia. There are inevitably stressful times and trips away with a project like this. I thank them for putting up with me throughout.

EXTRA BONUSES!!

EXTRA BONUSES HERE NOW!

We can't give you everything you need to know about franchising or growing your business in one small book.

So we've created a very special website with loads of extra **FREE** resources, just for you.

You'll find easy ways to get access to the amazing people featured in this book.

There are checklists, reports, tips and tools to help you grow your current business and ways to find out how to own your very own franchise.

Go Check out our Bonuses at:

www.FranchiseLeadersBook.com

CONTENTS

Foreword   1

Introduction   3

Jack and Melanie Harper – Franchisors of Driving Miss Daisy   5

Paul Bull – CEO of Signature Homes   17

Adam Parore – Franchisor of Small Business Accounting (SBA)   29

Scott Jenyns – CEO of Aramex/Fastway Couriers   41

Grant McLauchlan and Rene Mangnus – Franchisors of CrestClean   53

David and Karen Dovey – Franchisors of Exceed Franchising   67

Andrew and Denise Lane – Franchisors of Night 'n Day   81

Brendon Lawry – CEO of Liquorland   93

Gill Webb – Franchisor and CEO of Active+   105

Paul Jamieson – Franchisor of Kelly Sports and Kelly Club   117

Simon Harkness – CEO of Kitchen Studio   129

Simon McKearney – Executive General Manager of Helloworld New Zealand   141

Next Steps in Franchising – Simon Lord   155

About the Author   163

Contacting Our Contributors   165

Recommended Resources   169

New Zealand's Top Franchise Service Providers   170

FOREWORD

New Zealand is the most franchised country in the world. It's a fact that might surprise many people, but it's true. According to the 2017 Survey of Franchising conducted by Massey University, there are 37,000 franchised units in this country. That's one franchised unit for every 124 people.

Another surprising fact is that the overall turnover of the franchise sector is now estimated at $27.6 billion – equivalent to 11 percent of New Zealand's GDP. Add in motor vehicle sales and fuel retail, and it comes to $46.1 billion.

But perhaps the biggest surprise of all is that most of these franchises are not big international brands. When I founded Franchise New Zealand magazine back in 1992, franchising was a little-known concept in this country and we had just a handful of local operators. Today, over 70 percent of the 600-plus franchise brands operating in New Zealand are homegrown companies operating in all sorts of industries from home services to real estate, gourmet burgers to bookkeeping. Many have expanded overseas,¬ not just to Australia but to the USA and beyond, and some are truly world class companies.

How have we got to this stage? Well, overnight success takes time, as they say, but it also takes visionaries who can see the advantages that franchising can offer. Combining big company buying power and branding with individual ownership and capital gives franchise companies the best of both worlds – if they do it right. Building such a company requires not just a good idea but good advice, good support and great leadership.

In this book, you can read about how some of New Zealand's best-known franchise brands were developed. There are tales of triumphs and disasters, of challenges met and of lessons learned. Above all, there are examples of how franchisors and franchisees work together to drive those brands forward. I applaud author Pete Burdon and the contributors for sharing their stories.

I often speak to people who are in the early stages of franchising their business, and others who have just bought into a franchise. I tell them that the more they learn and understand about franchising at the start, the more they will understand what to expect and the greater the success they will enjoy. This book can play a valuable part in that understanding, and I hope that you will find it both inspiring and educational.

Simon Lord
Founder, Franchise New Zealand media

INTRODUCTION

Franchising in New Zealand and around the world is a sector that should be celebrated for so many reasons. It allows thousands of people to run their own businesses who would otherwise have to work for someone else. These people get to control their own destiny and realise the dream of self-employment with all the support of a head office team behind them.

It's also a massive contributor to the New Zealand economy, accounting for 11 percent of GDP and employing more than 120,000 people. This creates opportunities in so many areas of business.

Why have you bought this book? You may be thinking about buying into a franchise or you could have thought about franchising your own business. The other possibility is that you are already a franchisor or CEO and are interested in how New Zealand's top franchise leaders operate and how they've got to that position.

Whatever your reason, you're in the right place. All of your questions will be answered by these leaders, all of whom operate in different niches. You'll hear how they got into franchising, the challenges they faced and how they overcame them, right through to how they market their businesses and their advice for anyone considering a move into this lucrative sector.

They share their stories warts and all and I thank them for that. The book is structured so that you hear their words directly from them rather than a version that's paraphrased by an external author. They have been carefully selected because I only wanted the very top New Zealand franchise leaders to contribute.

Finally, if you are interested in finding out more about investing in a franchise, I'd strongly recommend those in this book. They are all highly successful and focused on supporting their franchisees (or franchise owners as some call them), as you'll see in the following pages.

JACK AND MELANIE HARPER

FRANCHISORS, DRIVING MISS DAISY

Jack *"I'd rather die of thirst than drink from the cup of mediocrity."* (Dad)

Melanie *"If it's to be, it's up to me."* (Unknown)

JACK AND MELANIE HARPER
FRANCHISORS, DRIVING MISS DAISY

The inspiration behind Driving Miss Daisy was Melanie Harper's Aunt Trish who lost the ability to drive after a bus accident. Melanie began to play the role of companion driver, transporting Trish to appointments and taking her shopping in Havelock North, assisting her every step of the way. This sparked the idea of offering a similar service to people across New Zealand and further afield.

Driving Miss Daisy was launched in 2009 by Jack and Melanie. Since then the franchise has gone from strength to strength. There are now 75 franchisees in New Zealand, around 40 in the United Kingdom and the business is about to open its doors in Australia.

Jack and Melanie are not only top franchise leaders because of the phenomenal growth of the business, but additionally because they successfully created a new industry and transport category and overcame all the legal and bureaucratic challenges that produces.

Driving
Miss Daisy®

How did Driving Miss Daisy begin?

<u>Melanie</u>: I used to drive my aunt Trish around on errands after she broke her leg in a terrible bus accident. She tried taxis but they never arrived on time and the drivers didn't help her with other tasks like helping her in and out of the car. So she gave up on taxis and asked me to help her. She was my inspiration for Driving Miss Daisy. I drove her for eight years. I loved helping her and we had fun when we were out and about. Sadly, over that time and from her perspective she lost her independence and felt indebted to me, so she stopped asking me for help so often and would opt to stay at home. Then one day her son suggested that she ask her neighbour Di to drive her and pay her for the service. That's exactly what happened. I could immediately hear a change in the tone of Trish's voice. This re-empowered her, gave her back her independence and let her plan the journeys just as she would if she was driving her own car. She was much happier and began engaging more in her community again.

This was my light bulb moment. I thought there must be a whole lot of people sitting in their houses here in Havelock North who would want to go out with somebody lovely. They would pay for the service, they would not be accepting charity and it would be on a commercial basis. I thought, I could be the "Morgan Freeman" of Havelock North because I visualised that the role was the same as that he played in the movie, as the servant/driver of Miss Daisy in Driving Miss Daisy. So, I thought I could have a business and call it Driving Miss Daisy. What a great name for a business. I would drive and assist my clients and they would design the journey.

I googled Driving Miss Daisy and found there was a franchise in Canada that already had the name and was doing a very similar thing. That's when Jack's light bulb moment hit. He thought we could offer to buy an Australasian Master Franchise. I told him to hang on a minute. I just wanted to have a little business in Havelock North that could make a difference in peoples' lives here where we lived, but his vision was much bigger than that.

Jack: To cut a long story short, we met the owner of the Canadian franchise and found that she had no desire to move into any other countries herself. I could see real opportunities for the business as a franchise. It was also great timing for me because I had just sold my financial planning business, the first one in Hawke's Bay, and I wanted to head down a different track.

We hired a business advisory firm to research the market here in New Zealand. They found that like everywhere there were taxis, buses, shuttles and various other options, including volunteers but there was nothing that offered an individualised, personal companion driving service. So we created a new category in the transport industry because there was no such thing prior to that. While that was good news, it also meant we had to educate the market, which itself is quite a challenge when you first start.

Melanie: The industry we started was companion driving. That's what we've called it. The driving is important, but that's only part of the service. It might be just a regular 'taxi' drive to the doctor and back. But then we can help them out of their house, take them into the doctor if they need the help and arrange a time to come back and pick them up so they don't have to ring and book another ride and sit around waiting.

Jack: While the service is about getting people from A to B, the companionship is number one. The reason that ninety percent of these people love going out is because they end up spending time with their Daisy who can, over a period of time, become like a surrogate daughter or a surrogate son. They long to see that person because on many occasions, it might be the only time they actually have a decent chat to somebody all day, or all week.

In hindsight, was franchising the best option to grow the business?
Jack: Absolutely because we knew that this concept had to be far bigger than Melanie in Havelock North. As I said to her, there are Trish's everywhere across New Zealand, there are Trish's everywhere across Australia, the UK and the rest of the world and no one's looking after them. So franchising was the logical model to help them and create a wonderful business opportunity for other people. It also meant that the people duplicating what we were doing would be highly conscientious because they would have a vested interest in their business as well as the brand as a whole.

What do you look for in these franchisees?
Jack: We needed to attract what I call 'Melanies'. The initial profile we developed was people somewhere between the ages of 45 and 60 who had perhaps been professionals in other areas, perhaps no longer had kids at home and would rather have their own small business than work for someone else. Like Melanie, we wanted people who were empathetic, loved helping others and positively impacting the lives of people in their communities, while building a business and asset for themselves.

They also have to be teachable. We've had franchisees who've never had any business experience before Driving Miss Daisy achieve phenomenal results. For example, our current Supreme Franchisee of the Year spent 25 years in a pharmacy before joining us. She had never owned a business of her own and she was somewhat nervous when she started, but we knew she had the teachability. She followed the system, asked lots of questions and now she's a successful business owner and she's developed a great team of local Daisy Drivers who she employs and who spread the wonderful service across their local community.

Melanie: It's also important they're IT savvy. They need skills to work with our system. For example, we have apps that we use on our smartphones that are vital to running the business. Our franchisees also need the ability to employ and build a team. We prefer franchise owners who are business partners together, so either a husband and wife or a couple of people doing it together. This works well because we find that it builds a good balance, with each focusing on their different areas of expertise.

What support do the franchisees get?

<u>Melanie</u>: Overall, we give conscientious support and mentoring for all aspects of the business and service. Jack and I, with our team at Head Office, are hands-on and focused on franchisee support with regular reporting and catch-ups required.

Our franchisees also use a booking and scheduling system with a database and that talks to Xero. Some of our franchisees don't know what a Profit and Loss Report is before they start with us, so we train and mentor them. We also have a section in our training on business plans and provide a business plan template. We require their completed business plan before they start and then modify it through the training if necessary. We also follow up on it annually.

<u>Jack</u>: The Operations Manual and the training itself was developed by us from the get-go. I remember when we wrote the manual. It said things like, "These are the activities you will put in place for marketing. We don't want anybody sitting at their kitchen table with a cup of coffee wondering why their phone isn't ringing. And these are the activities you must implement day by day, hour by hour." We also have weekly and monthly franchisee business monitoring/activity systems that franchisees fill out online. This is part of our accountability process.

Nowadays our Business Manager is talking to our franchise owners monthly and we also insist on a field visit with a structured agenda every year in their office for a good two or three hours. It's important our franchise owners see us face-to-face and this includes their attendance at our annual National Conference, which is compulsory.

(Melanie with the Hawke's Bay team of drivers)

Tell us about the UK operation?

<u>Melanie</u>: We sold what's called a Country Master License to a group in the UK. This includes our entire toolbox including the brand, the operations manual, the driver training manual, the website and our support. The only difference are a few changes in legal requirements between the two countries, otherwise the business is almost identical to the New Zealand one. The market is also very similar. It's interesting driving around the different locations visiting UK franchise owners. We constantly hear the same wonderful stories as we do here in New Zealand. Our clients across both markets have the same needs, such as getting from A to B with the assistance of a familiar face and helping hand. It's really a mini-me of our operation here. Currently there are around 40 franchisees in the UK and with enormous growth prospects given the population size.

What are your future plans?

<u>Jack</u>: In addition to the New Zealand and UK markets, I'd like to see

little blue Driving Miss Daisy cars driving around Australia, Europe, probably South Africa, the US, and maybe also places like India. We did have an inquiry from India about a Master License, but it hasn't progressed yet. In places like that there's a massive expatriate population, and probably more people than the entire population of New Zealand that need a service like this. So, the world's our oyster in a way.

We think 85 franchises in New Zealand is about the maximum needed, but that will depend on the market and population growth. We've got to satisfy the market demand, which is a combination of more franchises and existing franchises growing their vehicle fleets. We've got about 250 cars at the moment and there's no reason we couldn't double that number over the next three to five years.

Melanie: While all of these countries are on our radar, our most immediate focus is Australia. We have interested parties over there who have already bought the Country Master License. We're just completing the documentation with them. Then we'll roll out the system just like we did in the UK. The need across the Tasman is massive. We constantly have emails from Australians asking us when we will enter that market because they know people who are using us here in New Zealand and love it.

What marketing do you do?
Melanie: When we started and wanted to attract franchisees, we'd run small ads in the local newspapers. People liked the brand, they liked what they saw and they could see the need and opportunity. We also ran seminars. Today, it's slightly different. There's a lot of word of mouth and we use social media in terms of wanting to fill a specific location. We create specific strategies for each region that can include a number of marketing initiatives.

Jack: The marketing we push with the franchisees includes networking, flyer drops and the importance of building relationships. This last one is such a priority that we even take into account how long a potential franchisee has lived in the area because this can impact on how many existing relationships and networks they already have in place. Franchisees also contribute to a national marketing fund that we coordinate at head office to run TV campaigns, national radio campaigns and many other tactics to bring in business for our franchisees nationwide.

How strict are you about franchisees following the system?
Melanie: It's full-on. Our franchise agreement is very clear on compliance requirements. We have strict instructions about things as simple as how to greet people at the door. We have strict instructions about uniforms. They have to buy the cars that we provide. They also have to be on our telephone and IT systems. We're very systemised and strict about following the system. I think that's been the essence of our success and the growth of the brand.

What has been your biggest challenge?
Jack: In the early days, educating the market about what a companion driving service is was a huge challenge and sometimes we leveraged off the Canadian story. But now people understand what Driving Miss Daisy and companion driving is. Even government departments such as ACC and NZTA are putting companion driving services into their documentation.

It was a huge challenge at the beginning to educate Regional Councils and NZTA about what we did and the need for it. This was in particular when we applied to be part of Total Mobility Scheme, where those in need of transport assistance could get subsidies for using council-accredited services.

What made this more difficult was that every region had its own scheme definitions, meaning we had to approach each one individually. It took up to three years for some to accept us. This was frustrating for everyone, particularly our clients who needed us and couldn't receive the subsidised transportation. We're now in all but one region and our clients with a Total Mobility Card only pay half of the cost themselves up to a given limit, with NZTA and the local regional council paying the other half.

Melanie: Another big challenge is the cost of setting up a franchise. We funded the business ourselves and it always costs a lot more than you think. Franchisees also need adequate capital. They need the capital to buy a business and all the other expenses that go along with that like buying new cars and the marketing costs associated with attracting clients in the early days. Even though this is a lower entry cost than lots of other franchises, they still need to be well resourced.

What's the most rewarding part of your journey so far?
Melanie: It's definitely seeing the smiles on our clients' faces because our service has given them back their independence and provided them with companionship at the same time. For example, many of our clients live with dementia, but that doesn't mean they can't live in their own home and community happily.

There are many great home care services available these days but the problem for people is often getting from home to community activities. We're an important component for people living in their own homes. We're the conduit between home and their community involvement. It's well known and proven that anybody who lives with dementia or any form of disability is going to be healthier if they can get into the community and be involved with other people as they have always been. It's so satisfying to know that we are helping more and more people do that across the world.

<u>Jack</u>: Additionally, it's been wonderful to see a growing number of small business owners who buy a Driving Miss Daisy franchise go on to build a wonderful business for themselves, while contributing so much to their local communities, both as a service provider and an employer of numerous drivers.

What advice would you give someone who is looking at franchising their business?
<u>Jack</u>: Is there a market? Just because you've done a great job in your local town doesn't necessarily mean it's going to work everywhere else. If you're convinced there is, get quality franchise consultants to help you with the next step. Get a lawyer who is a franchising lawyer, not someone who says he's good, even though he's never dealt with a franchise. There are lots of lawyers like that. Be prepared to work 24/7 in the first few years and make sure you either already have great leadership skills or you develop them with help.

<u>Melanie</u>: Talk to other franchisors and join the Franchise Association of New Zealand. We're members and you should also be if you want to be a recognised franchisor. The most important thing to know is that you can't operate a franchise business unless you have 100 percent integrity. If you don't, it'll never work.

PAUL BULL
CEO OF SIGNATURE HOMES

*"If it doesn't make the boat go faster …
don't do it."* (Sir Peter Blake)

PAUL BULL
CEO OF SIGNATURE HOMES

Paul has spent most of his career in the building industry. He started in sales and operations before moving into senior management and governance roles. His wealth of experience, along with the excellent governance of owners Gavin and Anneta Hunt, has seen Signature grow significantly over the last five years.

Before taking up his current role, Paul could see how franchises in the building industry operated and what could be improved. This has seen a number of developments at the company including more training for franchisees and extra input from the Support Office into their businesses.

An interesting point about the growth of the company, both with Paul at the helm and before, is how well it has flourished without a significant increase in franchisee numbers. Paul and the Hunts have been primarily focused on helping the current franchise partners grow their businesses rather than expand the network. This has clearly been a successful approach.

Signature HOMES Est. 1983

YOUR HOME. YOUR WAY.

How did you get into the building industry?

This'll be my 30th year in this industry. I'm quite pleased and quite proud about that. I fell into it really. I studied architectural drafting, and then got involved with a landscaping business. From there, I moved into the building industry. I then worked my way up through primarily sales focused roles before deciding to move out of the sales arena into more operations and general management positions. That's what led me to my current role with Signature.

Tell us about Signature Homes

The company was founded in 1983 by Fletcher Challenge when it built solid wood homes. The components of those homes were manufactured at its Mount Maunganui factory and transported throughout the country. The business was sold to the current owners, Gavin and Anneta Hunt in 1995. It was in the 1990s that Signature moved into the 'design and build' market for the first time and also started building homes, commercial buildings and resorts around the Asia-Pacific region. One example was the Sheraton Bora Bora Resort.

The company flourished under the Hunts, including the export side of the business where it won the 1998 and 1999 New Exporter of the Year Award. It was in 2000 that the company set its sights on becoming New Zealand's leading home design and building group. It joined the Franchise Association of New Zealand (FANZ) in 2002 and won the Business Leadership Award at the FANZ awards that year. Over the next few years, Signature won some major public and private contracts including one to build over 100 early childhood centres across the country. The business continued to flourish. For example, in 2009 it built over $100 million worth of homes and buildings. Over the last five years, we've continued this phenomenal growth to the point where we now exceed $200 million in new homes annually.

What do clients get from Signature that they may not get from another builder?

Firstly, we're one of the oldest, if not the oldest, surviving building brands in the country. Our clients don't have to rely on standard contracts that build in cost overruns and unclear completion dates. We have our own contracts that guarantee there will be no cost overruns and that people can move into their homes when the contract specifies, not a day later. We've all heard stories about people having bad experiences when they build a home. It either costs more than originally quoted or it takes too long to complete. We know this is stressful and that's why we offer our own guarantees, which are the best in the industry in New Zealand. We want your home-building experience to be simple and exciting. Our guarantees are unique to the building industry in New Zealand and apply to all of our franchisees.

How does a building franchise differ from more traditional franchises?

The big difference is that our franchisees are selling a product that doesn't exist. You're taking large chunks of money off mums and dads and selling them almost a dream. So there's no product when they start to pay you big chunks of cash.

Typically, franchises sell goods and services and off-the-shelf products whereas housing or building is quite a complex sales and commercial process.

How does selling franchises differ from other industries?

Our model is that 'less is best'. At the moment we have 12 franchisees and we don't have ambitions to be the biggest and the broadest business in the country. We want 12 or 13 financially stable businesses. So when we are recruiting, we spend lots of the time finding the right partner who will tick all the necessary boxes. They need the right levels of capital, right vision of the industry as well as commercial experience.

How successful has the franchise been recently?

We've had a fantastic five years, effectively tripling the business in that time. The interesting thing about that is that we've only grown by one franchise over that period. Our progress has been focused around optimising performance at each franchise, and coming up with unique and localised strategies for each business to improve. To achieve this, we've basically become thought partners with our franchisees. It's more of a coaching and mentoring type relationship rather than telling them exactly what to do.

I was lucky to have sat in other CEO chairs in the building industry before joining Signature. From there I could see how franchisors related, communicated with, and led their franchisees. I think we've taken that to another level. For example, we have a full breakdown of their salaries, costs, expenses, cost of goods and where they're buying their products from. It's all totally transparent and we get a detailed health check of their performance every month. They effectively consult with us on everything and that's made our relationship really strong. I never saw that with other franchise builders before I joined Signature. I think this is all why we won so many franchise accolades at the 2016/17 FANZ Awards. That year we won:

Westpac Supreme Franchise System of the Year 2016/17
Winner – Signature Homes

Best Franchisee 2016/17
Winner – Vogue Homes Signature Homes Bay of Plenty Craig & Debbie Williams

Best Franchise System 2016/17
Winner: Signature Homes

Best Home Services Franchise System 2016/17
Anneta and Gavin Hunt of Signature Homes

(The Signature Homes team at the 2016/2017 FANZ Awards)

What has your focus been since becoming CEO six years ago?

I was lucky to inherit a business that had good systems and processes already in place. Apart from what I've just mentioned, there's been a big focus on improving our people. We've been recruiting excellent support staff and improved the training we offer everyone. For example, we've introduced communication training to all parts of our businesses. Not because they weren't communicating effectively before, but to create a best practice around how to say the same thing in a better way.

It's like the old adage, you can say the same thing two or three different ways. But if you say it better, it comes across better. It's also about how to have a courageous conversation with a client or staff member.

I also believe we're the only housing business in the country that has a true National Conference. We assemble 98 percent of our staff in Auckland every year. It's not just sales awards or construction-focused. It's everyone from front desk people through to the franchisees themselves. There's some celebration of roles and star performers, but primarily it's focused around how we improve as people. The focus of the conference is always about real personal development.

(Drinks at a Signature Homes Conference)

We've also introduced milestone reporting. That means each franchisee can see how productive they are with their time and learn from those who are outperforming them. This is great for the franchisees as well as the customers. That's because the shorter the duration of time between each milestone, the sooner they can move into their new homes. These results are all kept so that each business can see how well they are performing over a 12-month period compared to the previous year and compared to other franchisees.

Do you have any major goals for the future of Signature Homes?
We're not motivated by large audacious goals. We like to set a good plan for the next 12 months and then the following 12 months and focus

on achieving those goals. We want to make sure we don't bite off more than we can chew. It's important that we don't make promises to our franchisees that we may not be able to keep. The main focus will be to continue doing what we've been doing. We want to grow but we don't expect to keep growing at the phenomenal rate we have over the last five years.

What marketing do you do to attract clients?

We use quite a variety of marketing channels. We still use television advertising, some radio and local print media because that still gets read despite what lots of people think. We also have a focus on signage, but the big change over recent years is the move into the digital space. We use everything from electronic direct mail to Google AdWords. We've even started automated campaigns where we ask a number of questions and the follow-up people get is dependent on their answers. This is far more effective than generic targeting.

What's the biggest challenge you've faced and how did you overcome it?

It's probably moving out of a centralised office model with over 1000 employees into a company where everyone's an owner-operator. The big challenge with that was having to relearn how to sell and pitch ideas and initiatives, rather than just telling people it had to be done.

I had to soften my approach too. While it took a bit of time, the Signature family is a close-knit team and we communicate well together. If someone ever has a problem or they don't understand something, they don't hesitate to ring me.

What's the best advice you ever had?

A former boss once told me not to worry about what I can't control tomorrow, but worry about what I can control today and be urgent about it. That's great advice and something everyone should follow.

What do you think is the biggest myth out there about franchising?

I think there are some franchisors who just sell territories and cross their fingers that it will work out when they haven't properly vetted their franchisees or thought about the customer. That's what really stuck out to me about the Signature Group because I knew them well before I came on board. They were a client of mine. I liked the philosophies that Gavin and Anneta stood for and the support they gave their franchisees. They've really set the standard for that from a franchising perspective in the building industry and shown how well a franchise can perform when the focus is primarily on supporting the franchisees.

What advice would you give potential franchisees in the building industry?

These people have typically been owner-operators before so they're used to doing things their own way. One of the points we overpitch and over communicate is that you're joining a group that has done things a certain way for 30 years. We know what works and what doesn't work. So, we're not interested in people who are not going to listen. We did have one franchisee who wanted to do things differently like design his own signage. We had 30 signs to choose from, but he still thought he knew better. The point I'm making here is that if you want to do things your own way, rather than what's been proven, Signature is not for you.

But if you do like the franchise model, do your research. It's important to understand the brand you're talking to. Spend time to understand the people and the franchisor and see how they behave. Also speak to other franchisees in that network and make sure the systems and processes exist to support the brand. Then make sure the culture fits well with you.

(The Nelson Signature Showhome)

Is there a person you really look up to?

My focus has always been on the people in my immediate sphere of influence and using tidbits from each person I've worked alongside. I've learnt from all of my leaders including their positive traits, and some that are not so good. But I've looked up to them all.

I think we can all learn from the people around us and that's something I've always done. But I can't single out any one person who stands above the others as a leader I've respected the most.

What's the key to being a successful franchise leader?

Recruitment. Getting the right people in the right roles is the key to a successful franchise. If you get the right people on board, you can do anything. When it comes to the day-to-day stuff, having the experience and the proven systems and processes all really help. But unless you've got the right people executing, with the right level of urgency and the right level of passion, you can't grow anywhere near as quickly.

I think that's been the difference with us in the last five years. We've unearthed the entrepreneurial spirit of each franchisee and given them confidence because they've got a support office that's going to coach and mentor them to the highest possible standard.

Do you have anything to do with recruiting staff for franchisees?

Absolutely. Recruitment is just as important for them. We work with franchisees to get the best staff to complement their particular skills. For example, if a franchisee is strong in construction, we'll help them recruit staff with a sales focus, but if they're strong in sales, we'll help them recruit in construction. We stand beside them and also assess 90 percent of their staff. We're also launching a formal recruitment programme to teach them exactly how to find the right people.

Do you have a set of values that the company lives by?

We have important standards, but because they are so unique to us, we don't publish them. What I can say is that we've recently steered away from corporate-speak-like mission statements and vision statements. We've simplified it all to give our people a sense of belonging. We've come up with four simple standards that we call the Signature Standards. They're all based around people and how we want our people to behave.

We've been quite explicit about them. For example, we say, "This is Standard A. This is how you live up to Standard A and this is how you don't live up to Standard A." We've made it quite clear and quite precise.

ADAM PARORE

FRANCHISOR OF SMALL BUSINESS ACCOUNTING (SBA)

"Get up, dress up, show up and never, ever, ever give up."
(Adam Parore)

ADAM PARORE
FRANCHISOR OF SMALL BUSINESS ACCOUNTING (SBA)

Adam Parore is better known to many as one of New Zealand's best cricketers. He represented the Blackcaps as a wicketkeeper and specialist batsman between 1990 and 2002.

What fewer people will know is that he is now one of the country's top franchise leaders. He is the owner of Small Business Accounting (SBA) and also has other franchise interests outside that company.

Since purchasing SBA in 2008, he has grown it from 25 franchisees to 63 and has big plans for the future.

Adam says the key to successful franchising is finding quality people. He surrounds himself with the people he considers New Zealand's best business brains in their specific areas and gives them the autonomy to work their magic.

Adam has always valued being part of a team. This left a big hole in his life when he retired from cricket, but franchising has given it back.

Tell us about life when you pulled stumps on your cricket career?

It was pretty liberating for about two days and then it got a little scary. I was originally planning to be a prosecutor but when I found out how much a first year law clerk/junior prosecutor earned, I changed my mind. I followed my second favoured career, ending up at Goldman Sachs in the investment team. I did that for almost a year but never fitted into the investment banking type mould. Coming from a professional sporting background, the dealing room at Goldman Sachs was quite a culture shock. The personalities weren't what I was used to and it didn't have that sense of team about it. It was literally a group of individuals under a common brand. I also discovered pretty quickly that being an employee was probably not suited that well to me. I found that committing myself to one thing for 24 hours a day was difficult. I had done that during my cricket career, but now I had so many things I wanted to do. It was clear that having equity in a business was a way to have that flexibility I wanted.

Why the move to franchising?

My journey into franchising came about by a strange series of events. I bumped into an old friend, Stu Beadle, at a junior rugby match in 2000. Stu owned a cleaning franchise. Because the mortgage broking sector was strong at that stage, he suggested we open a franchise in this area to go up against Mike Pero. That's what we did and Adam Parore Mortgages was a success.

While my only understanding of franchising at that point was McDonalds, I can now see the obvious progression I took. That's because when I was playing cricket I also had a job as a marketing consultant at Coca-Cola Amatil. That's where I learned about brands and marketing, and that's the area I focused on in the mortgage business, while Stu took care of the franchising side. Our partnership worked well and I learnt about franchising from Stu along the way. It also gave me the flexibility I needed. I found that I related well to the franchisees because they were normal, everyday Kiwis who were similar to me.

Did you like the team focus that franchising offered?

Yes. It wasn't until I stepped away from that team environment inside the Blackcaps that I realised how important being part of a team was to me. I hadn't recognised that because it was all I'd ever known since I was five years old. But as soon as it was taken away, the camaraderie, the respect and the code of being part of a professional sporting team, it left a big hole in my life. You see this all the time in the media when players struggle to deal with retirement. Franchising gave some of that back to me in a way that Goldman Sachs never could. It also became clear to me that I'd learnt a lot from playing international sport that could be transferred to franchising. For example, building teams and commercialising skills into different areas.

When did you buy SBA?

Stu and I purchased SBA in 2008 because we saw it as a good add-on to the mortgage broking franchise. At that stage there were 25 franchisees. It was in pretty good shape, but we could see areas that needed attention. It was a bit like buying a nice residential house. The bones were there but we wanted to add a tennis court and swimming pool. In 2010 Stu moved to the US so I took over the business, running it myself for five years until I employed Craig Gardiner as general manager.

What has been your biggest highlight so far with SBA?

The transition onto Xero. This was a two-and-a-half-year change management process where we essentially bet the business on the belief that Xero software would be able to deliver better outcomes for staff, customers and improve the profitability of franchisees. I worked hard to convince everyone that this was the right decision. We literally moved somewhere in the vicinity of 12,000 to 15,000 customers from one platform to the other. It was a ground-breaking project in Xero at the time. It was a bit of a leap of faith and there was a group of probably half a dozen experienced franchisees who didn't want to change platforms because they'd been on the previous platform for 15 years and change isn't much fun. But my view was much grander, and the board supported me that this was critical, not only to continue to move the business forward, but for survival. In the fullness of time, the decision has been proved to be the right one. It was hard work and culminated in us receiving the Xero partner of the year soon after.

Has the support you offer franchisees changed?

Yes. It's hard to write franchise operations manuals that take an accountant or a bookkeeper through the process from the moment the customer walks through the door with a query through to the point of preparing their financial statements. That's effectively showing them how to run a business and how to be an accountant. We've found that the whole process takes too long. So we've recently come to the conclusion that the training on how to be an accountant or bookkeeper is best left up to professional bodies and by being supported by practicing accountants. We've found this leads to better outcomes for everyone. We still offer a massive amount of support and have a huge focus of consistently increasing what we offer our franchisees.

Is compliance with the IRD part of your franchisee support?
Absolutely. This has been a big focus over the last few years because our franchisees see one of their key risks being new people coming into the system and not reaching the standards that are required. That's why we support them all from head office by doing extensive compliance reviews, annually and bi-annually. We also have a dedicated training and support manager who is literally on the road 24/7, visiting each office, doing simplistic compliance. That's one area where we're different. Lots of franchise niches are unregulated, but our industry is not one of them. We need to audit from a regulator's perspective so we can foresee or front-foot any issues as early as possible.

We've had one or two issues over the years with noncompliance activities from franchisees, and we've learned that the process of managing them out of the business, and then satisfying the customer needs, is pretty traumatic for everybody. That's why we are now quite heavy-handed when it comes to making sure that every franchisee complies.

What's the biggest challenge you face?
Finding good quality people is always the critical component of any business, whether they be franchisees, employees, shareholders, or directors. This takes time. One thing I've learned is that labour, particularly management, is scalable. Nobody really talks about it. I

have people in my core group who are 25 to 30-year veterans in their areas of expertise. They are the best in the country at what they do. I've put them in environments where they are comfortable, given them autonomy, access to capital and they've achieved amazing results for the franchise. A big part of my role is finding these people and bringing them into the business either as managers, CEOs, directors, shareholders or some combination of the four. I'm not trained in their expertise, so they don't report directly to me. It's important for franchisors to find these people, trust them and give them control. Then they'll get you the results you need.

Another big challenge for any franchise is finding the right franchisees who can also finance their business. We've solved this to some extent by taking advantage of our own banking resources to arrange finance for them. That's one thing that makes us a bit different from other systems. If the right person wants to acquire a franchise, we'll go out and buy a practice and convert it to an SBA business for them and provide the money. This works well because lending into your own franchise network is a very secure loan.

(Theme night at an annual SBA Conference)

What are your future plans?

We've spent the last few years ensuring we have compliance sorted and making sure we have all the necessary systems and supports in place. Now the focus is on investing back into the network and helping the franchisees hit their targets. We now have 63 of them across New Zealand and we are looking to grow to 80 to 100 over the next three to five years. I believe that would be full penetration for a country the size of New Zealand.

We've also made a change in our approach that I call franchising 2.0. This doesn't only include SBA, but other businesses I have in my wider group that include a number of rental car franchises. With all the expertise we now have at board level, we're looking for ways to actually grow the network by establishing the businesses ourselves. We're looking to establish them, grow them to their first 25 to 50 clients, and then sell them to franchisees or continue to operate them. We're also looking to buy commercial property and develop sites for our rental car franchisees.

In addition to this, we're interested in taking a merger and acquisitions-based approach to building multifranchise systems because we've got the expertise and the experience to do that.

We've done this in Christchurch where my wider group teamed up with some entrepreneurial accountants to roll up nine accounting practices into one under the umbrella of Small Business Accounting South Island and move them into the SBA network. We're looking to replicate that model.

What marketing do you do?

We've always had good success through the *Franchise New Zealand* magazine. Lately we've moved online. The dynamic of the SBA franchisee is quite interesting. Often they'll see an advertisement and come in for an interview. They may then disappear for a period of time and walk back in the door 18 months to two years down the track. I'm not sure why that happens but I think its unique to the accounting niche.

How many of your franchisees had other accounting practices before SBA?

About 30 to 40 percent had existing operations that they wanted to scale up and could see the massive lead generation that SBA could bring them. Often they come to us with 25 to 50 clients and move that up to 300 to 500, which is where most SBA businesses sit.

What specific qualities do you look for in franchisees?

People who have the ability to be part of a team. I'm looking for those who want to be a part of something bigger than themselves. I'm NOT looking for star players.

What mistakes have you made?

In terms of day-to-day operations and stuff, we haven't had too many big disasters along the way. I mentioned earlier the importance of IRD compliance. We did have an issue with one franchisee being noncompliant. I think we moved too slowly and that's probably our biggest operating error. We were almost too trusting of that franchisee. We won't make that mistake again. In the end, that franchisee was terminated.

A big regret of mine is my failure to buy shares in Xero back before it got anywhere as big as it is today. I took a huge punt on it with SBA and that was clearly the right decision. But to this day, it amazes me that I saw the technology first, was that company's biggest fan for over a decade, and elected not to buy the shares at one dollar each. I think they're trading at $55 today. I was in the industry, I was an expert in software and picked the winner. I absolutely picked it and didn't put any money on it.

Do you have a mentor?

I've had a few over the years at various stages. Sir John Graham (Former All Black, NZRU President, Auckland Grammar Principal, Blackcaps Manager) was very important to me in my mid-20s when I had some success but needed to do a fair bit of growing up. More recently Stu Beadle has been a huge influence in both business and life generally. In many ways he's been the big brother I never had.

What advice would you give someone looking at franchising their business?

I think you need to be a little cautious to be honest. I see a lot of businesses that people mistake as being great future franchises. From my own experience, it's not easy to grow and develop a business that survives for 10 to 15 years, which is really what you need for it to be successful. And to be able to deliver value at every level is difficult. A lot of people take that for granted, but it's not easy. When I say sustainable, I mean that everybody needs to get fed. The customer needs to get value and get a service that they are happy to pay for at a price that they're happy to pay for it. The employees need the business to make enough money to provide them with a salary that's competitive in the market.

The franchisees need to be able to make enough money to justify the risk of being in business for themselves and provide a return on capital that's appropriate. The franchisor needs to make a margin on his or her efforts and capital. And don't forget the suppliers who need to build enough of a margin into their products to feed themselves. It's quite complex to get to the stage where it's completely sustainable and it doesn't happen in two or three years. It takes a long time.

The other thing to think about is how prepared you are to give away control. At its core level, franchising is simply another capital raising methodology. It's the same as raising equity through selling shares. In return for giving away a slice of your business, in the form of a franchise or shares, you're also giving away control. So there's a lot to think about before franchising your business. A lot of people I know are looking to buy back their networks. You can also see that lots of the systems being sold through New Zealand simply aren't sustainable. Franchising is a great sector in New Zealand, but it's not for everyone and will only work for select businesses. I can't emphasise enough the need to do your homework before considering the jump.

SCOTT JENYNS
CEO OF ARAMEX/FASTWAY COURIERS

"What we need to do is always lean into the future; when the world changes around you and when it changes against you – what used to be a tail wind is now a head wind – you have to lean into that and figure out what to do because complaining isn't a strategy." (Jeff Bezos)

SCOTT JENYNS
CEO OF ARAMEX/FASTWAY COURIERS

Scott Jenyns has had a busy few years. Not only has he overseen a company with 1700 franchisees across four countries, but he has been at the forefront of a massive rebrand.

Fastway Couriers has come a long way since it started as 'a man in a van' in Napier back in 1983. This success with Scott at the helm is why Dubai-based express mail delivery company Aramex purchased the company in 2016. Aramex operates in 70 countries across the globe.

Scott has led the rebrand, where the focus has been to communicate the message that the change has created a huge range of new opportunities for Fastway customers and franchisees, while maintaining the unique Fastway brand.

Tell us about the origins of Fastway Couriers?

The company was established in 1983 in Napier and is now a globally franchised courier company with a presence in New Zealand, Australia, Ireland and South Africa. It's come a long way from 'one man in a van' to a global franchise with over 60 regional franchisees and 1700 franchisees in the four countries mentioned. We now handle over 40 million deliveries every year.

Fastway was founded by Bill McGowan, who after completing sound research on the courier industry in New Zealand at that time, saw a gap in the market to establish a courier service that offered competitively price courier services between Napier and Hastings. It wasn't long after the company's inception that Bill decided to franchise. This allowed the company to expand the network and grow to the point where Fastway could offer services nationally.

The company started to grow rapidly on the back of setting up a proven franchising model that worked on a three-tiered basis. This comprised Courier Franchisees, Regional Franchisees and a National Master Franchise. The success of the business can be purely attributed to the franchise model that Bill initiated in 1984, after just one year of trading.

The Aramex purchase has provided the business, our franchisees and customers with access to world-leading services, research, resources and expertise. In 2019, the company embarked on a significant rebrand project that delicately balances and embraces change whilst respecting the company's proud history and brand reputation in both the franchising and courier delivery sectors in New Zealand.

What did you do before becoming CEO at Fastway?

I've played a number of roles at the company since joining in 2011 and I've been the New Zealand CEO since 2014. I'm also a director of all New Zealand companies operating under the Fastway, now Aramex brand. Prior to joining the company, I worked within the apple export market and before that I was based overseas in Ireland and the United Kingdom. I hold a Bachelor of Business Degree from Massey University.

Fastway was recently bought out by Aramex. How has that changed the business?

Aramex is considered one of the top five logistics providers in the world with a presence in 72 countries, transporting nearly 70 million parcels globally each year. That means we're gaining a global mindset with access to new innovations, new technologies and new shipping destinations. This is a major step forward for our local franchise operators and also for many New Zealand businesses that either export products to the world or import to New Zealand.

But just as importantly, we're retaining our industry unique franchise business model. That's why very little has changed since the sale to Aramex, apart from the very visible name and brand change. But it most certainly has opened up new opportunities for our franchisees with parcel delivery to and from international markets.

We've been able to launch international services on the back of the acquisition, whereas prior to Aramex, we were unable to do so cost effectively as we used third party service providers (effectively our competitors).

Our franchisees now have access to world class technology which is immensely important as technology continues to drive changes in the way we do business and how consumers buy products and services.

Aramex have an international franchise team so they have experience with franchising around the globe. They're also very supportive of investing in start-up businesses, which provides even more opportunities for our franchisees. That's because as new investments are made in a start-up business by Aramex in other parts of the world, we can assess whether there are synergies that can be applied to the New Zealand market to further improve our customers experience or add value to our franchisee businesses.

What is the biggest challenge this change created and how did you overcome it?

Whilst I'd say the challenges we faced weren't significant by any stretch, and the Aramex team have been immensely supportive throughout and continue to be, I would say we had two barriers to overcome. The first was that not many people outside the international logistics sector knew the Aramex brand. Secondly, with change always comes uncertainty from the people within your business including franchisees, employees and customers.

Overcoming that first challenge comes down to sound marketing principles and regular public relations. If the team have done their job properly by the time people are reading this, customers and potential customers may well have already had a parcel delivered by Aramex here in New Zealand. They're also likely to have heard about the brand through our various marketing and public relations activities.

To address the change anxiety created by the acquisition from the outset, we invited the New Zealand-based management team, all regional franchisees and top tier customers along to an Aramex roadshow where they had the opportunity to meet and greet the Aramex executive team in person. This was well received by all attendees and demonstrated that Aramex was here to support their businesses and franchises and offer improved services. For customers it was important for us to ensure they knew we weren't altering our franchise model and they'd continue to do business with a locally owned and operated franchisee.

What qualities do you look for in franchisees?

Attracting and retaining the best people is one of the core pillars to our mission of 'delighting the customer at the door'. We're always looking for the best people to join our award-winning team and share our success. Our franchisees come from all walks of life. Over the years, those who succeed are enthusiastic and energetic with a strong customer service focus and the desire to build a successful business whilst working within the guidelines of the Fastway franchise system.

We offer two franchise opportunities. A regional franchisee employs office and depot staff to provide support functions to courier franchisees in the areas of administration, operations, sales, marketing, technology and customer service. In other words, the regional franchisees offer total business management support which requires a skilled business person with strong business acumen, good leadership skills and the willingness to take a hands-on approach.

The courier franchisees own an exclusive territory within the area covered by a regional franchisee where they provide parcel pickup and delivery services. Under our model the courier franchisee owns the customer relationship and has the opportunity to build on their customer base within their exclusive area. They do this by leveraging sales support from their regional franchisee and the national commercial team who are always on the hunt for new nationally spread customers.

Tell us about some of the awards the franchise has won and what the judges said?
We're currently the proud winners of over 41 franchise and industry awards and our commitment to be the best we can be is the cornerstone of our continued success.

In recent times, the award that I'm proudest of, along with our team of franchisees and management, would hands down be the Community Involvement awards that we were presented with at the Franchise Association of New Zealand (FANZ) Awards in 2016 and 2017. When I talk to many of our franchisees I can hear a sense of pride in their voices from being recognised nationally for their efforts locally. It also reinforces in them that they're part of the Fastway/Aramex family, rather than just one person in a large business.

The Franchise of the Year judges said Fastway had learnt over the years the value of both its employees and customers, and how they all come together to make a community. "They have shown an ongoing commitment where they can both use national and regional initiatives to help others less fortunate or in great need," the judges said. The full list of our awards can be reviewed on our website at www.aramex.co.nz.

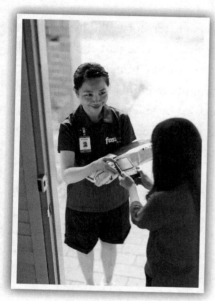

(The old Fastway uniform)

What's the biggest lesson you've learnt since being at Fastway/Aramex?

When I attended the Fastway couriers training course for the first time back in 2011, day one of a two-week in house course was conducted by founder Bill McGowan. He stood up and said to us all, "Do not trust anyone in business."

I thought at the time that this was quite a negative approach to take. However, I can assure you that after almost 20 years in the industry I've seen it all and have been let down by placing too much trust in people where reasonable sums of money have been involved. The sad truth is that money influences many behaviours and Bill was right. So make sure you have robust processes in place when recruiting franchisees.

These should include sound background checks and interviews, because when you grant a franchise to a new franchisee, as a franchisor you have a huge responsibility to your existing team of franchisees to protect the brand and avoid poor selection and the opportunity for a bad apple to damage your brand.

What's unique about the Fastway/Aramex franchise system?
Our franchise agreements are perpetual or permanent for both regional and courier franchise levels. This is quite rare these days with many franchise systems opting for license periods that expire and therefore require renegotiation.

Our system is also unique as our network relies on all franchisees playing their part within the service chain. For example, if a parcel delivery required input from franchisees in two regions and one franchisee delayed the delivery due to a service lapse, then the other franchisee could potentially lose the client. This creates is a strong peer support programme amongst fellow franchisees who will go out of their way to help support other regions that may need some specialist training and support from time to time. As a franchisor we welcome this and encourage regional franchisees to conduct visits to other regions to impart their experience and advice.

I draw similar parallels to the parent and child relationship. For example, when I was teaching my two children to ski they would never listen to me, even though I can ski well enough. But if another parent offered advice, it was completely different and they would respond positively. This scenario is common in franchising to help overcome this barrier to the franchisor–franchisee relationship. I recommend ensuring you have a balanced management team made up of experts in their field and in some cases former franchisees or business owners.

(The new Aramex uniform)

What are the most important things you've learnt about successful franchising?

Make sure you set up an active Franchise Advisory Council that meets regularly to share ideas on how to continue to evolve the franchise system. If done well, you can create an environment that's conducive to a more collaborative approach as opposed to draconian, which in today's business environment simply doesn't work. We've worked hard on this approach and whilst we don't always get it right and we can't always make decisions that please everyone, we're clear and honest on the decision-making process we take.

What are the common mistakes made by franchisors and franchisees?

I always say to the management team and franchisees that success always starts and ends with recruitment. If you get your franchise selection process right and attract the best candidates, you're already on your way to running a successful franchise. But if you take shortcuts and don't abide by sound and proven recruitment selection processes, it can end up costing your business and brand reputation in the longer term.

As a franchisor the selection of your management team is also vitally important. Ensure you have a diverse range of skills and experience within your team. I personally find that managers who've operated a franchise before are more widely accepted by franchisees when conducting on-site visits. They also tend to offer the exact level of support franchisees are seeking because they've walked in their shoes. This helps to avoid the parent and child scenario mentioned earlier and helps to avoid conflict often seen in franchise systems whereby field managers assume they have too much authority over a franchisee. Franchising isn't like a traditional corporate structure. I've seen great managers who possess excellent skills totally miss this point and struggle to operate in a franchising environment.

What advice would you give someone who is considering investing in a franchise?

We encourage our potential franchisees to meet with and talk to existing franchisees and not just the one they're buying from. This way they get a balanced view of the opportunity. I would also reinforce the importance of research. This is simple these days because most research can all be done by your fingertips with a quick Google search.

I also believe it's important that any franchise system you're looking at in New Zealand is an active member of the Franchise Association of New Zealand. This provides you with the added peace of mind that you're dealing with a reputable franchisor that's known to the association and abides by their strong code of ethics.

What advice would you offer someone considering franchising their business?

You can never do enough research on the sector and market you're looking at. So investing in a good research company to help you would be a must for me. Make sure you seek sound legal advice on your franchise agreements using a legal firm that specialises in franchising.

I strongly believe that it's fundamentally important for you to own and operate a successful flagship operation that you can demonstrate the success of to current and future franchisees. This provides your business with credibility and reinforces to your team of franchisees that if you follow the franchise model, your business has a much higher success rate than not. It also provides for a great training facility for new franchisees.

GRANT MCLAUCHLAN AND RENE MANGNUS

FRANCHISORS OF CRESTCLEAN

Rene *"You can have everything in life you want, if you will just help enough other people get what they want."* (Zig Ziglar)

Grant *"My biggest success in business was the discovery some 40 years ago that by attracting excellent people to work with me and giving them a chance to grow, I would go much further than I would by myself."* (Jorge Paulo Lemann)

GRANT MCLAUCHLAN AND RENE MANGNUS
FRANCHISORS OF CRESTCLEAN

CrestClean was one of the first franchises founded in New Zealand and has been the clear leader in commercial cleaning for many years. It was established in Dunedin by university friends Grant McLauchlan, Rene Mangnus and David Marsh in 1996.

The company faced some difficult challenges in its early years, mainly because very little was known about franchising in New Zealand at the time. Since then it has grown massively and now supports more than 630 franchise teams involving over 1800 people who service more than 5000 customers nationwide.

Grant and Rene stand out as franchise leaders for a number of reasons. For example, not only have they created a highly profitable business for everyone involved, but they guarantee the income of their franchisees.

CrestClean®

Tell us how the partners came up with the idea of a cleaning franchise back in the 1990s?

Rene: I met long-time friends David Marsh and Grant at Otago University in the 1980s. They were locals and I was from Tauranga. We all came from entrepreneurial families and all knew we wanted to be business owners. David had already started a part-time video rental business and I launched a word processing service after I saw my grades rise when my papers were typed.

When I met Grant at a party, we bonded over a common interest in surf-lifesaving. We went on to win a national championship together. That's where we learnt a lot about how to work together and a big reason why we're such an effective team in business 30 years later.

Following our graduation, Grant and I spent some time travelling and talking about what else we might do together. We went to Bali, Singapore, Thailand, Amsterdam and London and what we saw in all these different places were branded Western businesses. At the time Pizza Hut and McDonald's were all we knew of franchising on Kiwi soil, so we began investigating why franchising wasn't really a word in New Zealand.

Meanwhile, David had been living in London where he noticed lots of advertisements for cleaning contracts. He had an interest and understanding of commercial cleaning because his family was in the property industry. In 1992, he joined me for a trip to the Sydney Franchise Expo. We pulled a lot of pamphlets and brochures, talked to a lot of people and came back inspired. From that point on, we knew we should do something in franchising.

<u>David</u>: The more I got into property the more I could see the upside of cleaning as a franchise-based business. If you have someone who owns their business, they have a vested interest in looking after their customers because they want their business to succeed. Plus, if they're in uniform with a sign-written van and they're licensed and security vetted, those are details that impress a landlord. At the time, other cleaning companies weren't doing any of that.

<u>Grant</u>: We weighed up the pros and cons of various trades and commercial cleaning kept rising to the top. It was a large industry, had reoccurring revenues under contract and didn't require franchisees to sign leases for retail or office space. Furthermore, the New Zealand industry was dominated by foreign-owned corporates with high employee turnover. Standards were slack, wages terrible and training non-existent. The 'mum and pop' businesses existed on the periphery of the industry, but too often lacked the systems and business savvy to succeed. The size of the market was $760 million in 1996 and well over $1.5 billion today. That meant there was ample opportunity for growth.

So, in December 1996 we purchased a small Dunedin cleaning business, made the existing owner our first Master Franchisee and financed our first ever franchisee in the business as the pilot operation. Both stayed with CrestClean for many years and proved that the franchise business model that exists today is sustainable and delivers equity to all people involved, franchisees and customers alike.

What challenges did you face in those early days?
<u>Grant</u>: We realised early on that we wanted to grow a large and reputable business, so we had to fund expenses like systems development and branding well in excess of what our early revenues could afford. In year one we made a small profit, but for the next four years we experienced trading losses that really stressed our business.

Finding enough capital to grow was a constant challenge, as was our commitment to pay our franchisees every two weeks, even if customers hadn't paid their bills. Banks were tough to get loans from because franchising was so unknown, while an attempt to get investment from the capital markets didn't work.

After scraping some funds together from friends and family, we received a phone call from former airline captain and career investor, Tom Enright. He had seen our share offer in the *New Zealand Herald* and agreed to invest $100,000. After we met, Tom told us he invested because he thought we were quality people and believed we would do exactly what we said we would do.

Rene: This led to more equity investments that enabled us to move into the North Island, as well as establish Franchise Finance Limited in order to offer finance to good hardworking franchisees who for many reasons hadn't had the opportunity to save any money. We've since helped hundreds of people into business. They've paid back their business purchase finance and have gone on to buy a home, all from the cleaning industry.

Meanwhile, we developed a crucial banking relationship with Martin Hannagan at the National Bank. Martin could see the potential in CrestClean and was a great supporter of ours. This was so important because it was almost impossible to get most bankers to look past the balance sheet in those early years of franchising in New Zealand.

How has franchising changed since the 1990s?
Grant: Franchising has become more prevalent, more popular and certainly more accepted in the financial world and on a street level. It does sometimes have a negative reputation where big corporates leach away profits and provide little to zero support for their franchisees. We've created a different system that supports our franchisees, ensuring

they earn enough to achieve their business and personal goals and they have ample opportunities to grow and develop with the best tools and skills training they need to succeed.

How is CrestClean different from other cleaning companies?

Rene: We're all about ensuring the success of our people at all levels in the organisation. Some other cleaning companies take a lot less care to support and resource the operations team. There's a high staff turnover in the cleaning industry, as much as 100 percent per year, whereas the average franchise tenure with CrestClean is north of five years. That statistic says a lot about people relationships.

We can confidently say that CrestClean is the industry leader around innovation. A lot of people think of the cleaning industry as a last resort option for people between jobs, whereas we see it as a great opportunity to be a service provider. New technologies are being developed all the time and robotic and battery powered devices are making the job easier. We've led the industry in bringing environmentally sustainable processes into our day-to-day cleaning and this has certainly brought health benefits to our personnel and customers alike.

Grant: We've made it a central effort to raise the standards and status of the industry. We were one of the first New Zealand cleaning companies to sign-write vans, which brought positive attention to a hidden industry, plus it gave us free advertising via the rolling billboards and a good buzz as more and more vans popped up on Dunedin's streets after we launched.

Though CrestClean is a private company, when accountancy professor Marty Perkinson was appointed as our independent chairman, we adopted, on his advice, the governance practices of a publicly traded corporation. This has worked extremely well and adds great credibility to what we do.

Tell us more about the training you conduct?

<u>Rene</u>: By 2007, as we moved into our second decade of business, it became clear that more formal training was crucial to franchisee success and customer satisfaction, but there was a real lack of industry training in New Zealand. To fill the void, we established Master Cleaners Training Institute as a fully owned subsidiary, with its own CEO and a mission to 'raise the status and standards of New Zealand's cleaning industry'. The Institute leads a team of highly qualified regional trainers recruited from the most successful CrestClean franchises. This allows us to 'promote from within' by having our best franchisees train our future franchisees.

(CrestClean franchisees attending induction training facilitated by Master Cleaners Training Institute)

<u>Grant</u>: We've instituted mandatory training programmes, complemented with annual upskilling and including optional specialist skills training. We've seen lots of positive benefits from this. These include a drop-in contract termination, an increase in the average length of franchise ownership and a growth in the average franchise size as owners feel more confident in their abilities and more eager to turn their CrestClean businesses from side endeavours into full-time careers. We have franchisees who started with nothing, who needed business loans just to scratch together the initial $30,000, who are now running almost half-million-dollar businesses.

What exactly does the business offer?

<u>Rene</u>: CrestClean offers good hardworking people a full-service business system that enables them to achieve success, not only in business, but in their personal goals as well. Our people don't just make it in this economy – they thrive. We have new franchisees able to purchase homes in the high-priced Auckland region within just a few years of starting out.

How does your franchise system work?

<u>Grant</u>: We operate a three-tier franchise model. Firstly, there's CrestClean as the Franchisor. Our support centre in Dunedin provides all the essential business needs, such as customer invoicing, GST and financial accounts preparation. This is conducted alongside our marketing office in Mount Maunganui, which manages all of our advertising, brand development and marketing communications. We also operate a distribution centre, providing all the chemicals, uniforms and cleaning systems to franchisees.

The second tier is our Master Franchisees who buy the rights to operate the franchise system in a specific region. A Master Franchise provides a management level opportunity for a person or a couple to lead the business within a region. They represent CrestClean, promoting our services to customers, and also recruiting and managing our franchisee team.

The third and really important tier covers our franchise businesses. Our system stands out amongst others because we guarantee our franchisees an agreed amount of revenue, made up of a portfolio of cleaning contracts. That means we find them the work rather than just give them advice about how to find it. We then support and mentor them to become successful business owners.

Franchisees own their vehicles, cleaning systems and equipment. Because CrestClean looks after all the bookwork, they can focus on delivering excellent customer service and growing their businesses. CrestClean encourages and supports franchisees in gaining additional customers to grow their business and developing new income streams by becoming specialists in skills such as Hard Floor Maintenance, Carpet Care, Pure Water Window Cleaning and Property Caretaking.

(Tauranga Carpet Care franchisee Victor Haup with his specialised vehicle and equipment)

What specific support do you give your franchise owners?

<u>Rene</u>: We call ourselves a 'full service' franchise system. Within the franchise fee, CrestClean's support centre provides all the bookwork and compliances that frustrate most small business owners. Things like invoicing the customer, remitting payments to franchisees, initial and ongoing training, health and safety compliances and environmental compliances are all offered within a culture that's designed to foster success. Not only does the training ensure our people are technically competent to deliver a high standard of service, but it teaches them productivity gains and efficiencies when servicing their customers.

The relationships they develop with regional trainers, regional managers and our quality assurance co-ordinators provide multiple avenues of communication if people have questions or are experiencing unexpected issues or situations.

Grant: Our marketing office is constantly seeking new industry innovations, field-testing new equipment and chemicals and working with the manufacturer of our custom chemicals so that our franchisees are on jobsites with the latest and greatest in safety gear and tools. This foundation of support allows our franchisees to just go out and do a good job, get to know their customers and have the energy and capacity to go above and beyond and create a 'wow' factor with their services.

We believe we're the only franchise that provides actual accounting, preparing GST returns and the filing of tax returns. Whilst there are other franchises that have varying degrees of support, they don't do that service. We also act as a tax agent and we have a dedicated account manager at IRD.

What are your highlights over the life of CrestClean?
Grant: Working with hundreds of people who have never had the opportunity to apply their best abilities to achieve goals. Seeing how really nice people who may have been kicked around or let down in employment develop into successful business people through our training and mentoring. Seeing them take control of their own destinies has been the over-riding highlight.

Witnessing the joy on franchisees' faces when achieving home ownership – something that was beyond their wildest dreams prior to buying a CrestClean franchise – is also a priceless highlight. Home ownership by our franchisees is a strategy and KPI we celebrate often as it provides a huge amount of security and stability to families.

Rene: Another highlight was rolling out our Health, Safety and Environmental Management System, SafeClean®. When we saw that government was planning to create new rules and mandates around workplace health and safety, we closely monitored those developments and put the system in place at every franchise well before the new laws were introduced in 2015. The health, safety and wellbeing of our personnel has always been a top priority for us. It also meant we were able to continue with business as usual while other companies were caught out unprepared.

What are the plans for the franchise?

<u>Rene</u>: We believe we've developed a business system in a large and secure industry that can deliver great opportunities to all sorts of people. Our plan is to continue to do that. We have 53 nationalities involved in the business. Our youngest franchisee was 18 years old when he purchased his business and our oldest was 80 when he sold out, so we're an attractive business proposition to all. We also have a number of innovations we're pursuing, particularly around technology. Battery powered cleaning equipment is now being deployed nationwide and robotics is going to be a feature of our future. Smart machines have the potential to really lift the productivity of our franchisees.

What do you look for in new franchisees?

<u>Grant</u>: We seek honest hardworking people who are ready and willing to commit to our mission and adopt our culture of success. We'll take a chance on someone if we think they have the character to succeed. We have franchisees with all sorts of different backgrounds and we've worked with and tailored different size businesses and finance packages to get them started. There are very few costs associated with operating a CrestClean business and that means the profitability is quite high.

What marketing do you do?

<u>Rene</u>: Marketing has always been crucial. The vision of the company was to grow an iconic New Zealand brand in the cleaning industry and

to do that we spent a lot on marketing and other costs when the business was small. We continually devote significant resources to developing our brand, innovating our service offerings and refining the ways we talk about CrestClean.

In 2014, we started devoting more resources and attention to social media. In 2016, we successfully achieved an Environmental Choice New Zealand licence for our cleaning services and products. We are one of only two cleaning companies in New Zealand to have this third-party accreditation. This allows us to market with the ECNZ logo, showing our customers, franchisees and the public that we take environmental responsibility seriously.

Our marketing must be twofold. Firstly, to customers seeking cleaning services and to potential franchisees interested in purchasing a business. That's why our marketing office maintains multiple advertising platforms and online communication systems, including crestclean. co.nz, our main customer website and crest.co.nz, our franchise website with unique landing pages for every region.

We have also created RecycleKiwi, which is a public education programme to help improve waste management in New Zealand. RecycleKiwi helps schools to improve their recycling efforts with interesting and fun educational resources that can be viewed and downloaded at recyclekiwi.co.nz. Connecting with our customers and our communities in different ways is an important part of our marketing mix.

Our greatest assets are our people and we strive to share our franchisees' successes and reward them for outstanding work. This includes tenure milestones, such as a $2500 bonus at the ten-year mark. In advertising campaigns, we also use franchisees as the personnel as much as possible. This is to honour them as real people. They get a kick out of seeing themselves in the newspaper or online.

What would be your number one piece of advice to someone considering franchising their business?

Grant: Some people think franchising is easy because you get other people's money and you make money, whereas it's far more complex than that. Franchising is all about the benefits of scale and the ability to share the fixed expenses required to be successful. It's a huge investment to establish the structure, compliances and strategy to fund the growth. To do this usually costs far more than people think and takes way longer to succeed than they plan. Even as a franchise system starts to make a profit, there's a huge amount of capital needed each day to keep things moving.

What advice would you give someone who is considering investing in a franchise?

Grant: Like buying any business, do your homework, talk to existing franchisees and make sure you fully understand what you're investing in and what you'll get. We have a no surprises policy where we disclose everything so a prospective franchisee knows exactly how it all works. Look for a robust franchise system that provides comprehensive support. That makes good sense for everyone because it's in the franchisor's interest to make sure the franchisee succeeds. A franchise is a partnership so make sure you have common goals and that you can work together. Creating a win–win relationship is what you want.

DAVID AND KAREN DOVEY

FRANCHISORS OF EXCEED FRANCHISING

David *"Who am I if I don't make things better?"*
(From the movie *The Kingdom of Heaven*)

Karen *"Stay positive – you become what you think about."*
(Earl Nightingale)

DAVID AND KAREN DOVEY
FRANCHISORS OF EXCEED FRANCHISING

Husband and wife team David and Karen Dovey are the owners of Exceed Franchising. The multi-award-winning company is the industry leader in fixing doors and windows across New Zealand.

The seeds of the franchise were sown in 1990 when David formed Window Maintenance Company. After five successful years, the Doveys decided to franchise their concept. In 1997 after two years of hard work developing their system, Exceed Franchising was born.

The focus of Exceed has always been to treat franchise owners like family and to make customer service the absolute number one priority of the franchise. That's why David and Karen have limited franchise owners to 27, all with large areas to service and an absolute commitment to their customers.

Tell us about your working background before Exceed

David: I've been involved in the aluminium window joinery industry since the early 1980s, winning awards for workmanship and sales along the way. The key to my success was a total commitment to the customer. After that I took some time out to do the 'Kiwi OE' and spent four years travelling through Europe. For two of those years, I worked as a charter yacht skipper. During that time away, I could see that business success wasn't about driving people, but leading by example and encouraging others to follow. That's the way I liked to work and I'm sure that' a big reason why I ended up in franchising. When I got back from my big OE and started settling down, friends kept asking me to do their maintenance jobs. That's what led to the formation of Window Maintenance Company in 1990 and eventually Exceed Franchising.

Karen: I trained as a schoolteacher when I left school and soon moved into sales. I then worked as a hostess during my OE with David. The experience I got from those roles has been helpful throughout my time at Exceed. I joined David in the business back in 1993 when I started developing the Exceed Franchise system. I then left Exceed for a few years to start my own retail franchise before returning.

What exactly does Exceed offer clients?

David: While tradespeople don't have a great reputation for reliability, that's always been a high priority for Exceed. We know people call us when they have a problem and they want us to fix it for them with minimal hassle at the specified time. That's what we do. I think most tradespeople focus purely on the job they are doing, without necessarily giving a highly focused customer service. That's where we're different. We've stopped using language our clients couldn't understand, simplified our logo and always aim to exceed the client's expectations. That's why 'Exceed' is our name.

How does the service clients get from Exceed franchise owners differ from non-franchised competitors?
Karen: It's simple really. It's the core values that were developed by our franchise owners. These are reviewed with them every two years.

The core values are:

- The franchise owner will arrive on time or will call prior to advise
- We will do everything to provide an awesome service (for example, our free-call customer care centre)
- We will always smile
- We will always be well presented
- We will always wear a business ID for customer peace of mind
- We will wear yellow shoe covers in homes
- We will put down a yellow drop sheet
- All work will be labelled
- We will vacuum clean after jobs
- We will guarantee work unconditionally
- We will have a clean and organised van

In a nutshell, everything has always been entirely focused on the customer. We were also the first company in our industry to require police checks on all staff, the first to have uniforms, clear van signage and online interaction with customers.

How does your franchise system work?

<u>Karen</u>: Our system is designed around a small number of territories so we can give our franchise owners the time and commitment they need. Our focus isn't on selling more franchises, but helping our existing franchise owners grow.

Exceed has:

- An advisory board and management team dedicated to moving the system forward
- An advisory council of elected franchise owners
- Taskforce teams who trial new things before launching them to the group
- Roadshows for practical training and group togetherness
- Conferences for strategy and development
- IT support and development

What specific support do you give your franchise owners?

David: We've always looked at Exceed from the perspective of the franchise owner. The first question we asked ourselves was, "What does someone who has never been in business need?" That's why we have a large support office, high success rate and low exit rate. People perform better if they don't have to do everything and in small business that tends to be what happens.

Karen: With the changing demands of the industry and our strong focus on our franchise owners, we've expanded our Support Office to 18 people looking after our 27 franchise owners. Roles include IT, marketing, business mentoring, product knowledge and delivery and call centre support. This means we have control over the system and all the information our franchise owners receive. It also means that everyone is consistently going in the same direction.

The services you offer are very niche. What benefits/threats has this created?

David: It means we have quite large territories for each franchise owner. We see that as a benefit because we never wanted lots of franchise owners, but a small number that we could help grow. Another positive here is that because we're niche, we are known as the experts in what we do. This is even recognised by other companies who people may think are our competitors. They know that little mistakes when fixing doors and windows can be costly, so would rather use us to make sure those mistakes aren't made.

Karen: The large territories can also be a threat because if a franchise owner doesn't conform or grow, it can lead to a big hole in the market. We've had two situations like this where franchise owners weren't performing and tried to change the system.

But due to our constant monitoring and quick legal action, we were able to stop them. We were thanked by the rest of the team because their reputations were also on the line.

What would you say are the highlights of your time with Exceed?
<u>David</u>: The biggest reward has been watching franchise owners come in with no knowledge and seeing them evolve into confident and competent business people. For example, our second franchise owner, Paul Kelly, did all the right things when looking at the system. Firstly, he did his homework. He did lots of research before he interviewed me! I went up to see him in my suit and tie and he tested me to see how far I'd go to support him in business. He took me around his lifestyle property, moving cows and getting a reluctant pig past an electric wire. I must have passed because he's still with us today and has his family involved.

Family Involvement
We were based out of a home office for years because we wanted to have a good work/life balance and I think we got that. We had our children with us at Exceed conferences and working in the business. We loved having them involved, but as they got older it was no longer our decision. We're lucky that our son is now part of the business and he worked his way in. We didn't employ him. He turned up one day without our knowledge to be interviewed. There are always challenges having family in the business but when they can prove themselves over and over again, it's a great feeling. This 'family' base has been core with how we interview and take on franchise owners. If a partner isn't part of the interview, we don't accept them. We've even been marriage counsellors with franchise owners going through rough patches. We've supported them as much as we can and they've all stayed with us.

<u>Karen</u>:

The Christchurch Earthquake

The Christchurch earthquake had an impact on our franchise owners and our challenge was how we could support them. We realised it wasn't just about us but everyone in the system. We sent out a call asking who could help our Christchurch franchise owners and we had an amazing response. Everyone was ready to take time out of their own business to work within the Christchurch franchise. This was over months and took lots of pressure off the franchise owners in Christchurch to allow them to focus on themselves, knowing they had a business to come back to.

Changing support needs

As Exceed has grown, so has the support we've needed to offer. While some people may see that as a hassle, we've seen it as positive because its proof the business has reached another level. Let me explain. In the beginning, we needed more franchise owners, so that was our major focus. But once we had them on board, they needed the technical knowledge of how to fix windows and doors. Then as our need for more franchise owners diminished, the ones we had needed more technical knowledge and support in how to run their businesses.

At each level, we've been fortunate to have wonderful franchise managers. Ron White's ability in the technical skills area was second to none, Ron Houben was equally effective in sales and finding new products, while Tony Burnette is now doing fantastic work around how the franchise owners can grow their businesses. This is satisfying for us because most of our franchise owners are no longer a 'man with a van' but larger businesses with multiple vans.

Australia

By 2015, Exceed had really moved forward and we were looking at where to take it next. We looked at rolling out other Exceed brands like Exceed Home Painting. But just as we started that process, we were approached by a large Australian company, Doric. They had a business called Lock & Roll that was almost identical to Exceed, but it wasn't profitable. They asked us to help. Eventually, we spent a year documenting a franchise system for the Australian market. It's too early to tell how successful Lock & Roll will be in Australia, but it's looking good. That project obviously allowed us to move into Australia and was another example of how far we had come since those early days in the 1990s.

Tell us about the awards you have won

<u>Karen</u>: We've won lots of franchise awards, but it's important to point out that these are all a reflection of our franchise owners, because without them, we couldn't have achieved what we have. It's also been rewarding to see so many of them receive their own awards for their own businesses.

Exceed has won the following awards:

- Franchise Association of New Zealand (FANZ) Home Services Franchisor and Franchisee of the year multiple times
- FANZ Media recognition and FANZ media promotion
- FANZ Digital Innovation
- FANZ Franchise Manager multiple times
- Westpac Local awards in media marketing and business delivery

(The Exceed team wins another FANZ award)

How has franchising changed over the last 28 years?

<u>Karen</u>: Some changes in franchising have been positive and others negative. The systems are now better and more focused on the needs of franchise owners and helping them achieve their aims and dreams. But on the negative side, some people think franchising has become an easy path to expansion and they do it for reasons of self-interest and leave a trail of destruction. Luckily, they are the minority.

What vision do you have for the future of Exceed?

<u>David</u>: To continue to grow at the same pace it has done with us at the helm. We want it to provide ongoing opportunities for people to grow professionally and personally. It's grown exponentially from the beginning when it was 'a man in a van'. We want every franchise owner to have multi-vans so they have a strong business to sell when the time's right.

What marketing do you do and how has this changed over the years?

Karen: One thing that's never changed is the importance of word-of-mouth. Apart from that, marketing has been an evolving and constantly changing space. When we started, marketing was all about networking, flyer drops and yellow pages advertising. In the early years, the Yellow Pages bought in about half of our work. With the growth of the internet and social media, our reliance on printed media is almost nil. Networking is still key but the digital space is where we've made huge inroads.

What is the biggest challenge you've faced and how did you overcome it?

David: In 2002 we entered into a business partnership with a respected player in our niche. We saw this as a way to take Exceed to the next level. What we didn't know was that our new partner was about to sell off itself to a massive international player in the industry. This initially seemed good for us because most of the directors of the company we did the deal with were still in place. It also seemed that our plans to expand into Australia and further afield could be realised sooner than we planned.

Karen: But after a few years, the directors we knew all left and the remainder didn't seem to understand our business. After more discussions, the best way for Exceed to move forward appeared to be to sell the entire business to the international company. We would still be Exceed, but they would own the business. That's what we did but after 12 months, nothing had happened. This was when we bought the whole business back off them. We did this for a lower price than what we had sold it for. This was a stressful time, but things have moved forward significantly since then.

The Recession

With 25 years in business we've been through the good times and the bad. Thankfully, we got through the recession well. Thanks to our business partnership with Westpac, we had a really clear picture of what was coming and prepared well for it. Because of this planning, Exceed actually grew during the recession.

What's the best piece of advice someone has ever given you?

David: A business mentor of mine, Paul Dunn, gave me the best ever advice. He said if you give total focus to the customer, you'll need wheelbarrows to carry the money home. Our focus on the customer is our philosophy and that's why we are the leader in our industry.

What are the biggest mistakes made by franchisors?

David: Not letting go and trying to manage their franchise owners like employees rather than business owners. Yes, there is a system to follow, but once they have the system, allow them to run their business. Some franchisors also think it's a money bath and they can sit back and do little, while franchisees pay them for the privilege of using their brand. You have to be everything to your franchise owners. This includes being a mentor, marriage guidance counsellor, headmaster, financial whip and big brother, but not their friend.

What are the biggest mistakes made by franchisees?

Karen: Some don't do their homework before we interview them and don't always know what's involved in being a franchise owner. That's why we make them complete work experience days and take a specific test to ascertain their suitability. We also insist they seek professional advice before committing to anything. For the work experience day, we get them to go out with an existing franchise owner or two before they're rated. We've refused people because they either lacked the skills or their customer focus wasn't up to it. One appeared to have everything, but on the work experience day we found out he had a fear of heights and couldn't get past the second step of a ladder. Another was so shy that he couldn't even talk to a customer.

Do you have a particular person, current or from history who you look up to? If so, who and why?

Karen: Simon Lord (Franchise NZ Media and former Chair of FANZ) because of his dedication to the franchise sector over the years and the knowledge he shares. One quote I always remember from Simon was, "Look after the people who look after you." There couldn't be a better quote in franchising.

As a leading franchisor, what is the most common question you are asked, and how do you answer it?

David: People often ask me how they could franchise their business. I tell them this is dependent on two specific things. Firstly, is it franchisable because most aren't. If it is, the next vital thing they need is staying power, because it's a tough job to franchise a business. It creates lots of challenges and costs along the way. Most people looking into franchising also don't realise that everything they do needs to be written down so it can be followed by all potential franchise owners. We spent two years writing before we sold our first franchise.

(The Exceed team at a national conference)

What are the most important things you've learnt about successful franchising?

Karen: To be successful in franchising you need to understand that it's not all about the franchisor or the franchisee. It's about the culture, the development and the ability to work with likeminded people who share ideas and support each other in a strong business environment. That's why we believe this story isn't about David and myself but about all the people who work with us. It's about trusting all these people to deliver your message and that's only possible if they're dedicated, have had excellent training and continue to receive ongoing support.

What would be your number one piece of advice to someone considering franchising their business?

David: Talk with other franchisors in a similar structure to the one you're considering to get an impression of the impact franchising will have on you personally. It's a marriage you're getting into so compromise and a focus on success for all parties is important. This is quite different from a standard employer/employee relationship.

What advice would you give someone who is considering investing as a franchise owner (franchisee)?

Karen: Understand that it'll be hard work and make sure you have the finance to buy in and the confidence that it's right for you.

ANDREW AND DENISE LANE

FRANCHISORS OF NIGHT 'N DAY

Andrew *"The more successful a franchisee is, the more successful the franchisor."* (Andrew Lane)

Denise *"Stack 'em high and watch them buy."* (Ken Stevenson)

ANDREW AND DENISE LANE
FRANCHISORS OF NIGHT 'N DAY

Andrew and Denise Lane launched Night 'n Day Foodstore Limited in 1990 after 12 years in the convenience retail industry. With the national support centre in Dunedin, the company now has 53 stores spanning the length of New Zealand. The growth has been so phenomenal over recent years that Night 'n Day has scooped multiple Fast 50 business awards over recent years in the Otago/Southland region and this year was New Zealand's nineteenth fastest growing company among all-comers. This is an amazing result.

As one of New Zealand's first homegrown franchises, Andrew and Denise have successfully grown Night 'n Day over the last 30 years, despite many changes in economic conditions and customer tastes.

Night 'n Day has become the leader in the convenience store market because of its commitment to franchisee support and intense monitoring of trends to ensure it always has exactly what customers want, when they want it.

When did you launch the franchise?

<u>Denise</u>: We've both always been in retail, even before franchising. Andrew went straight into it from University and I owned a typical corner dairy. That's where we met and decided to go into business together in 1979. Soon we had two stores which we later sold to buy our flagship Dunedin store. This was the first one in New Zealand to be open 24 hours. After launching a few more locations over the next few years, the franchise was founded in 1990.

Why did you decide to franchise?

<u>Andrew</u>: We met the owner of an Australian convenience store franchise at a conference in Auckland in about 1989. Rod Craig had 19 stores around Australia and suggested we look into franchising our business. No one knew much about franchising in New Zealand at that stage so we did our due diligence. We could only find one person in New Zealand who consulted on franchising. This led to a three-day meeting with him and two other advisors from Australia.

One of our reasons for franchising was how it could remove us from the day-to-day running of a business, which freed up a lot more time. It also freed up capital, because we wanted to do all these amazing things but there was only a limited amount of funds.

<u>Denise</u>: Another factor in our decision was the slow demise of corner dairies. They were on a downhill spiral and we didn't want to be known as a dairy any longer. We wanted to be known as a brand that people could recognise. We wanted that brand to be known for its high standards and we couldn't see that happening as a standalone corner dairy.

What were some of the big challenges in the early days?

Andrew: A big challenge was establishing the system. That meant bringing all the systems that Denise and myself had together in our heads and writing them down in the form of a franchise operations manual. We'd never had a manual until then. I think anyone would find when you do this you change lots of things about how you operate and fill in any gaps. It's a huge job.

Denise: Finding people to invest in the brand was a challenge because we were unknown and so was franchising in the early 1990s. This changed in the late 1990s because we started moving into main streets in the cities. This gave us so much more recognition as a brand because until then our stores were mainly in suburban areas. It was like having massive brand billboards in the CBD.

How has the franchise changed over the last 30 years?

Denise: About five years ago I had to take one of my original delis out of a Dunedin store and replace it with a new one because it had been there for almost 30 years. That was the only thing that was still original. Nothing's the same as it used to be. The food we sell now is totally different to what we stocked 30 years ago.

We started with a small office. We did all the financial accounts ourselves, the GST returns, the PAYE and we ran the stores as well. Our role has changed considerably. I don't get as 'hands-on' in the Flagship Dunedin Store as I used to and that was something I enjoyed.

I'm now focused on supporting our franchisees. In the early days it was about trying to get good managers and maintaining the stores. When there weren't many of them it wasn't so hard, but when we franchised and got bigger, that all changed. Our focus had to change because there were so many more day-to-day things to deal with. When you've got 53 stores, franchisees often want to do something different. Trying to keep them consistent and maintain the brand is more of a challenge now than what it was back then.

<u>Andrew</u>: I think everything has changed, and most things have changed multiple times over that three decade period. There's been a lot of progression in all aspects. Our product has changed, our point of sale and payment methods have changed, the market has changed and so has how we market the business. We always monitor trends nationally and internationally to keep up with the market. We also like to bring in new concepts that are outside what's been traditional convenience retail. We like to distinguish ourselves from supermarkets and petrol stations, as they also change. For example, ten years ago supermarkets wouldn't have served barista coffee.

(Inside a Night 'n Day store)

How well do you work together?

Denise: I work more on the operations side of the business. I like to be in the stores, laying them out and bringing in new products whereas Andrew looks after the financial, legal and leasing areas. We learned early on that we worked best when we had our own areas. Going back, he would do the drinks, and I wouldn't touch the drinks. I'd do the confectionary, and he couldn't touch my confectionary. So we've always split the roles even though they have changed a lot.

How has the family fitted into the business over the years?

Denise: We've got four children and they all loved the flagship shop in Dunedin. We used to live behind it. They all worked in the shop to pay their way through university, because we had a standard rule that if they failed they had to pay us back the fees. They're all still involved with Night 'n Day, some heavily. Our oldest son, Murray (42) owns two stores in Dunedin, our second oldest Korina, is our national operations manager while our youngest son Matt is now our general manager. Our other child, Katie, has her own legal practice, but still does some work for us. We're extremely proud of them all and so happy to have them all involved. They know the business better than anyone because they grew up in it and worked in the business for so many years during their educations.

This family focus has also extended to our first franchisees. Our first three are still with us and two of them have sons who have bought their own stores. One has two and is looking at a third.

What qualities do you look for in potential franchisees?

Andrew: Just good motivated people with good ethics, good manners and tidy working habits. We don't have a preference whether they're qualified or unqualified. We've got everybody from former office workers to spark technicians to senior police officers. They come from all walks of life. What we don't want are people who are too independent and want to do things their own way rather than what the system says and has proved successful. They also need to be prepared to work long hours and have a passion for their work.

What support do you give your franchisees?

Denise: We offer comprehensive support including a full accounting service. We have four chartered accountants in our office who do all the financials for every franchisee. We take that right out of the store so they concentrate on retailing while we focus on the corporate side. This also means we know exactly how successful they all are and if there's anything we need to work on with them.

Tell us about your Fast 50 Awards

Andrew: The Deloitte Fast 50 is into its nineteenth year in New Zealand. It recognises the country's fastest growing companies based on their revenue growth over the preceding three years. We were so proud this year to be New Zealand's nineteenth fastest growing company. This is a phenomenal result when you consider how many companies there are across the country. It's a credit to our entire team. We've also won multiple first place awards in the lower South Island section of the Fast 50 over recent years.

The Fast 50 Results for Night 'n Day

2012. New Zealand's fastest growing company for retail or consumer products in the lower South Island

2013. The fastest growing mature business in the lower South Island

2018. The fastest growing consumer business in the lower South Island

2019. The fastest growing retail and consumer products business in the lower South Island and nineteenth fastest growing company across New Zealand.

What are your future plans?

<u>Denise</u>: One of our main plans is always to have our existing stores continue their growth. We don't have to add numbers for the sake of adding numbers but we do want to grow over the next five years after a period of consolidation. After appointing Matt as general manager, I've got no doubt that will happen. We'll also be rolling out new concepts again this year. We haven't done too much of that in the last 12 months because it's a lot of work for the franchisees and we hit them so hard with a whole new food rollout last year.

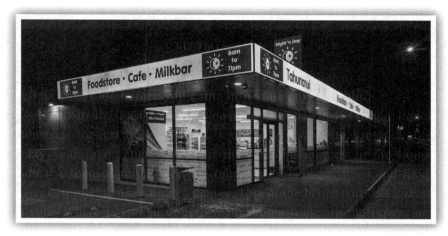

<u>Andrew</u>: Another focus that we've started is helping our franchisees manage change. We've had lots of feedback lately that one of their biggest problems was the amount of change that was happening. And it was impacting on their lifestyles.

For example, the whole training system has changed. It's all online now and we're wanting to do more training around all the different areas like health and safety and marketing. We also changed all of our coffee machines and revamped our food offer. This can really disrupt the day-to-day operation of a store. Everything we've done in the last 12 months has been innovation to make change easier. We'll keep up this focus in the next few years.

What marketing do you do?
<u>Andrew</u>: One unique thing we do is partner with different real estate agents and business brokers. This helps when a franchisee may be looking at selling and when we're looking to build our own green field stores and selling them as businesses. We also work with existing store

operators who are not part of Night 'n Day with a view to converting them into Night 'n Day franchisees. For example, we offer them our training module on how to deal with an armed robbery. We're looking at expanding this part of the business. The beauty of assisting them is that we want to help, but it also demonstrates our expertise and increases the possibility that some may want to convert their businesses into Night 'n Day stores.

When it comes to marketing to customers, we're heavily involved in social media. For example, we have 60,000+ Facebook followers and we've maintained that for many years and our fans there do a lot of the work for us. We also advertise on television and radio with MediaWorks. On the local front, the franchisees control that. They do things like sponsor the local school newsletter and advertise in community newspapers. We also supply them with merchandise like sports bags and other promotional products.

What advice would you give someone who is thinking about franchising their business?
<u>Denise</u>: Pay for the advice you need and do the job properly because it's a huge move and it's not right for every person or every business. Also make sure you document everything you do and speak to other franchisors and the Franchise Association of New Zealand.

(The counter inside a Night 'n Day store)

Are there any myths in New Zealand about franchising, particularly after the bad publicity in Australia?

Andrew: I don't think so. I see where Australia has gone wrong and it's not because of myths, but a few crooks. The sector's taken a real hammering over there and people are staying away from franchising. It'll take time to repair its reputation.

Denise: Unfortunately the Australian situation has made people a bit reluctant over here because it doesn't do the franchising sector any good when we hear these negative stories no matter where you are.

What's the highlight of your time with Night 'n Day?
Denise: For me, it's a couple of things. Firstly, its going into sites and seeing the improvements and the satisfaction from the operators. Also watching the second generations come through as I've already mentioned. Some of those franchisees were born into Night 'n Day and

now have their own stores. But just seeing the franchisees getting a good return back and enjoying themselves is the biggest reward for me.

<u>Andrew</u>: Denise has nailed it. Seeing healthy franchisees who are enjoying their journey with the whole system working for them is so satisfying. It's even more special when we think about how long so many of them have been with us. The other highlight for me is seeing the impact of what we do for our communities. For example, a franchisee recently sent me through a picture of the kids he'd sponsored with big smiles on their faces while carrying Night 'n Day sports bags and drink bottles. Those things are special.

What mistakes have you made?

<u>Denise</u>: I don't think we've got a big thing that we'd class as a mistake, but one thing that proved to be wrong at the time was our decision to put a coffee machine in our flagship store in Dunedin in 1992. This concept was about three years too early because people weren't ready to buy takeaway coffee. We'd take it out of the store for a week to use at our annual conference and there'd be no drop in sales. It cost us $10,000 and made about two cups of coffee a week. But after those few years, things started to change and making coffee is now a major part of our business.

BRENDON LAWRY
CEO OF LIQUORLAND

"Don't just aim for the next job, set your sights on what you ultimately want to be capable of."
(Peter McClure, former boss)

BRENDON LAWRY
CEO OF LIQUORLAND

Brendon Lawry has established himself as a franchise leader after more than 20 years in the Fast Moving Consumer Goods and Liquor industries. His management focus has always been on meeting people's needs.

He emphasises that the big distinction with franchise leadership is the addition of franchisees to the people mix and the importance of looking after their needs as much as customers.

Brendon says that selling alcohol comes with a huge responsibility and that's never far from his mind.

Liquorland has over 120 stores across New Zealand in an industry that's highly competitive. There are more than 1000 outlets that sell alcohol across the country. While this creates its own challenges, they pale into insignificance when compared to Brendon's successful fight against cancer four years ago.

LiquorLand

Tell us about life before you came into your current role?

I've been in the Fast Moving Consumer Goods (FMCG) and liquor industries for just over 20 years. I started my working life as a chef many years ago. This kicked off my learning journey in the liquor industry, focused initially on the relationship between wine and food. After completing a commerce degree, I spent the better part of 15 years in roles where I worked directly with the customer in the liquor and dairy sectors. After having had the major retailers as customers for so long, when the opportunity presented itself to join them, it was too good to turn down.

How does a liquor franchise differ from franchises in other niches?

My deduction is that the success factors don't differ that much. At its core Liquorland, and I think most business (retailing and service industries in particular), are in the people game. Our customers, competitors, suppliers, staff and franchisees are all people, and the better you understand people, the better you understand business.

One of the key differences in our sector is the legislation specific to alcohol. This is the Sale and Supply of Alcohol Act. We treat a liquor licence as a privilege rather than a right. Selling alcohol comes with a huge responsibility and this needs to be respected. While it's true that the grand majority of Kiwis have a healthy relationship with alcohol, some sections of society don't and that's why the retail sale of alcohol needs to be taken very seriously. As a consequence, we have a number of policies, procedures and costs that are unique to liquor stores and liquor franchises.

The traditional liquor retail sector including bottle stores and supermarkets is also incredibly competitive. There are well over 1000 retail outlets in New Zealand selling alcohol.

Tell us about Liquorland and how it's different from other liquor businesses?

We differ a lot from the remainder of the Liquor industry because of our Foodstuffs relationship. As the franchise is owned by the North and South Island Foodstuffs co-operatives, we get all the advantages you might imagine from being part of New Zealand's largest retailer. They are like the ultimate and wise big brother who is there to help when you need it, and not get involved when you don't want their help.

We gain leverage through the size and scale of Foodstuffs. This includes their experience and expertise with retail systems, IT, legal and training opportunities for our franchisees and their staff. We also benefit from the buying leverage. The greatest advantage is the involvement in the work in putting the customer at the front of our thinking. Collectively we interact with over 1.5 million people per day. This gives us great insight into the dynamics and behaviour of the New Zealand shopper and consumer that our liquor competitors simply don't have access to. This helps us shape our offers, pricing strategies, build the right capabilities and really understand what people want when they come into our stores.

What awards has the business, or you, won?

The accolades I'm most interested in are the ones we receive from our customers. We implemented a customer feedback programme asking customers to email or text in their views on us and score us out of 10. Since its introduction we've had thousands of pieces of feedback and we constantly sit with a satisfaction rating of over 80 percent. Retail benchmarks in New Zealand mean that this puts us in the top five percent.

While we don't always get it right, we do most of the time and reading the comments from real people about our franchisees and their staff delivering a great experience is very satisfying. Often New Zealanders are quick to tell you why they don't like something, so when they tell you why they do like what you are doing, it makes it all that little more worthwhile.

On a personal note, I was inducted as a "Keeper of the Quaich" recently. It's recognition of services to, and work for the Scottish whisky Industry. There are only 2800 of us around the world and to be called out and inducted in a ceremony in Scotland at the end of last year was a career highlight.

What would you say are other highlights of your time with the business?
One of the highlights has been the changes we implemented to our operating model. This has seen us giving profits back to our franchisees, meaning we have moved more towards a cooperative model. This has helped us strengthen our supplier programmes, improve the profitability of our franchisees and strengthen our advantage in the market.

As a leading franchise CEO, what is the most common question you are asked, and how do you answer it?
I'm often asked, "How much money will I make?" to which I generally answer, "That depends how much effort you put in." There's no denying our business is hard and competitive, particularly because our product offer is generic, meaning you can buy Heineken and Chivas Regal in almost every bottle store in the country. But what we know is that the more you focus on, understand and look after your people including franchisees, customers, suppliers and even competitors, the better you will do.

Are there any little-known facts about the liquor industry that would interest readers?
I'm not so sure about little known, but almost every civilisation in the world worked out how to make alcohol pretty early in their evolutionary

cycle. Be it from grains, grapes, flowers, potatoes, citrus fruit, berries or famously getting the bread recipe wrong that created the world's first beer. As such the history involved in the liquor industry is incredibly deep, and global, be it 200-year-old distilleries or 800-year-old wine cellars.

Many of the world's largest brands remain privately owned, and have been passed down through generations, and as such the care taken by the people involved is immense. It makes for a very special industry to be involved in. The passion you see from people in the liquor industry is impressive, and hard not to get excited about.

Does the liquor industry get a bad rap and is it fair?
In many respects it does. The anti-alcohol lobby groups would have you believe that we are all drug dealers trying to create a culture of addiction. The media stories are often spun in a sensational way without showing a balanced picture. Sadly (like all sectors) there are people and organisations in our industry who don't operate with the levels of care we set ourselves, and as always, it's the small minority behaving badly who give the rest a bad reputation.

Yes, we sell alcohol, but the grand majority of New Zealanders have a healthy and responsible relationship with it. There is no doubt that some sectors of society need to be looked after when it comes to alcohol related issues and we work hard to ensure that we treat our liquor licences with respect. We always understand that our liquor licences are a privilege, not a right.

Most of the people in the liquor industry really care about the health and wellbeing of New Zealand and do everything they can to ensure all the obligations under law are met and people are looked after. We make decisions every day that no one sees that stop products coming to market that are incorrectly targeted or marketed poorly. We also invest heavily in responsible drinking programmes and work across the different industry groups focused on how we can reduce alcohol related harm.

What vision do you have for the future of the business?
I'm excited about the future of Liquorland. We set out a couple of years ago with a clear purpose to deliver the most successful, sustainable and responsible liquor retail environment in New Zealand. I believe we've already achieved that. We've also set up a great platform for growth that I'm confident we'll capitalise on over the next few years to see the Liquorland brand grow to absolute market leadership in terms of size as well.

What specific traits do you look for in potential franchisees?
We look primarily for franchisees who get the people game. We want them to understand that success will come as a result of the experience you create for the customer, and how you look after and manage other stakeholders including staff, suppliers and authorities.

It sometimes sounds a bit clichéd, but it's the size of your heart and the strength of your character that matters, and that's definitely true in a retail environment. Having talked to so many retailers over the years and walked the floor with so many owners, you can quickly get a sense of people's commitment to the customer experience. If potential franchisees don't mention the customer in the first few sentences of our discussion, it's unlikely that they would fit the type of person we're looking for.

It's a preparedness to care enough to properly listen. That's how you can spot the good retailers against the rest. They understand what it takes to enable their staff to be great, and they can articulate what they need to be able to offer the customer the experience they deserve.

What can you offer franchisees that others can't?

We offer a full service and independent franchise operation with the backing of New Zealand's largest retailer. We have a proven track record of success, a network of successful franchisees and support from the franchise office that provides a full promotional programme, strong supplier agreements, a full marketing programme across digital, social and traditional media channels, data analytics and in-sights, and importantly an operating model that shares profit with the franchisees.

What marketing do you do?

It's easier to say what we don't and that's largely television advertising. Given the rules around when you can be on air with alcohol, reaching our targets cost effectively is a challenge. Outside of that, we do the following:

- bespoke promotional campaigns
- we operate our own category magazine (*Toast* that is distributed with *Dish* magazine)
- we operate a digital platform across the major applications including Facebook, Instagram and our own website
- we still run a traditional printed mailer to 80 percent of New Zealand households
- we operate our own wine awards programme, (led by one of the country's most prominent wine judges)
- we have a number of sponsorship properties with three large beer festivals across New Zealand each year (Great Australasian Beer Spectacular (GABS), Beervana and the Dunedin Beer and Food show)
- We are the only liquor retailer that offers Fly Buys and Airpoints reward points and redemptions

What is the biggest challenge you've faced personally and how did you overcome it?

I'm a lucky survivor of cancer. I say luck because despite what people say, I reckon it comes down to luck. You hear people say they survived because they were determined, took a positive approach and never gave up, but you know what, some of the most positive, determined, strong people I have ever met are no longer with us and I am. I think I was positive, determined, and never accepted cancer was going to kill me, but no more than others I met. It's luck, plain and simple. I met two gents who had the same cancer and discovered it at the same stage I did. One was 10 years younger than me and the other 10 years older. Sadly, neither of them is with us anymore, and I can tell you they were as determined and positively orientated towards beating cancer as I was.

Once you have something like cancer give you a wake-up call, work challenges take on a new meaning and are very easily solved.

What do you think is the biggest myth about franchising?

That it's easy and you can take the procedures and processes designed by the franchisor and simply paint by numbers to a successful outcome. It's true that a good system combined with the right retail location is the perfect combination. But you have to work it, wrap your hands and your heart around it, care enough and fight to deliver the best customer experience you can.

Do you have a particular person, current or from history who you look up to? If so, who and why?

I don't have one particular person. I love learning from people and I have a number of people I use for guidance. Some have become friends, others formal mentors, and others don't even know I take much notice of them. People in this last group are typically the ones I make a point of doing the opposite of what they do.

I've always enjoyed reading biographies and have read a huge amount over the years. I find myself fascinated by the lessons of war. I can't really imagine it personally, but I'm sure the enormity of leading men and women into battle focuses your mind on strategy and leadership in particular.

I've read and watched a lot of interviews with General Norman Schwarzkopf. He wasn't everyone's cup of tea, but I think a lot of his wisdom is applicable well beyond a battlefield. He talked about character, clarity of purpose and principles. It's hard to argue that all of those things aren't important in any business and leadership role. But it's amazing how many people claim to have all three, but when you apply a small amount of temptation or pressure, you learn that they have none.

What are the most important things you've learnt about successful franchising?
It's all about the people and experience is the key driver of success. It's also vital to get the right balance between the support office and the franchisee. Neither can do it all on their own.

How do you see the future of franchising in New Zealand?
I think it has a bright future because the New Zealand culture suits franchising. It promotes local ownership, rewards hard work and enables creativity without needing to risk everything. That's assuming the operating model is strong.

What would be your number one piece of advice to someone considering franchising their business?
You need to really understand why your business is successful, how you make money and what your strategic advantage is. That sounds simple, but a deep understanding of why things work is often harder to

understand than why something failed. Once you understand this, you need to work out how to replicate it. Then support, guide and coach new people towards delivering the same outcome.

You also need to be aware that everything you do in terms of operations, your business model, approach and customer plans can be copied. If you have specific intellectual property, invest early to make sure it's protected.

The next and most important thing is to focus on your brand, not your logo, but what people say and feel about the business. Brand reputation and health is crucial. Your brand is the thing that can't be copied, but it can be beaten. As such it's important to think about what sort of people you want involved in the franchise because they will be part of your brand story. Have a very robust selection process.

Don't be afraid to say no to potential franchisees because having the wrong people will create the greatest distraction, most brand damage and cost you and the business real money.

What advice would you give someone who is considering investing in a liquor franchise?

Do your homework. Don't just look at the model, the cost, the financials and the historic performance of the business. Talk to the franchisor and make sure that their approach, strategy, business plan and importantly their character and integrity match yours. Talk to current franchisees and not just the ones the franchisor tells you to talk to. Lastly, remember it's a people game, and success comes from your people. If you don't like dealing with people, franchising is probably not for you.

GILL WEBB
FRANCHISOR AND CEO OF ACTIVE+

*"Every accomplishment starts
with the decision to try."*
(Hilary Clinton)

GILL WEBB
FRANCHISOR AND CEO OF ACTIVE+

Thirty years after it began as a small one room physiotherapy practice in Central Auckland, Active+ has become one of New Zealand's largest multidisciplinary rehabilitation suppliers.

When Gill first put that sign out on Manakau Road in 1990 following six years working overseas, she had a vision to change the way physiotherapy was practiced. In those days the term was loosely defined and hugely variable between practitioners.

Gill's vision was to move the focus away from the use of machines on patients to identifying exercise and client participation as the cornerstone of recovery and long-term benefit.

The early success of the business led to Gill employing a number of associates, followed by the opening of other practices around Auckland. The next progression was to franchise the business.

Active+ is unique in the market because it doesn't only offer physiotherapy, but the full range of rehabilitation services such as occupational therapists, psychologists and medical doctors.

The business has come a long way since 1990. It has 660 clinicians and a growing franchise base of more than 20 that span from Northland to Manawatu.

Tell us about your career before Active+

My interest in physiotherapy began when I played representative netball as a teenager. From the age of about 16, we had physios involved in our training and injury management. They were great people and really switched on. They were a major reason why I went straight from secondary school to physio school. Following graduation, I worked for a few years in Palmerston North and then five years overseas. Soon after my return, I met a young GP in 1992 who was setting up a practice in Epsom and was looking for a physiotherapist. I worked long hours and the business grew strongly through the support of the GP and word of mouth. In 1994, I moved across the road to a bigger space and started employing likeminded physiotherapists as associates. Over the following five years, we established six sites across Auckland.

Why did you decide to franchise the business?

The idea initially came from a client who was franchising a business across New Zealand and Australia. He was talking to me about what he was doing. At that stage I hadn't really heard much about franchising. That's where the idea stemmed from and funnily enough, one of his daughters, who was a physiotherapist, became one of our first franchisees.

After his introduction, franchising seemed like a great way to brand our style of physiotherapy because it was different from the norm in those days. The approach that was very much pushed at that time was using machines to do the work that could supposedly mimic what manual therapy would do. For example, electrotherapy pushed electric currents through the body to stimulate nerves and muscles, even though there was no firm research to show that it worked. This machine focus got to the point where you'd be so busy putting machines on people, you'd hardly have time to talk to them. So my generation of physios decided to go back to hands-on massage and manipulation, which were the roots of our profession. Franchising would also allow us to systemise processes so the public could be assured of a certain and consistent standard of service. Lastly, we already had multiple sites and associates who were looking for their own business opportunities but wanted to remain under our umbrella.

What challenges did you face in those early years?

One challenge was my role in the transition and the change in how physiotherapy was practiced. One of my roles within the profession was chairing a committee that was setting quality standards for private physiotherapy practices, because until then, there had been none. People could just about do anything and call it physiotherapy. There was no guidance for the public or for the profession as to whether that was best practice or not. So a collaborative approach with a number of the other key leaders in the profession came together and we wrote these quality standards. They were eventually bought by ACC and later used by Standards New Zealand. These standards became the basis of our franchise system.

Another challenge was getting away from the perception that 'one size fits all'. This is where we are different from lots of other types of franchises. People don't come in one size and people delivering the service have different approaches. So the systems need to be flexible to enable physios to do their best work for their clients.

It's not like making pizza but I think there is a perception that if you come and join a franchise physiotherapy practice, you'll be told what to do, and you can't do anything else that you think will add value to that therapeutic approach. That's not how we work.

Where do your franchisees come from?
Our early franchisees were our associates, so that was easy. We don't actively advertise, but we do make approaches to people we think would make great franchisees. Lots of these already have their own business. We also get approached by interested people outside of the physio profession.

Our first non-physio franchisee was the receptionist at our Albany clinic. She basically ended up running that branch when the then franchisee purchased another site and was spending minimal time at Albany. The concern was that the clinicians could feel a lack of leadership if the business owner wasn't a clinician. But we put in some clever systems around having their senior clinicians be supported to play more leadership-mentoring roles than they would if the franchisee had been the clinician. So they've adapted the systems to allow that to happen and it's been really successful. After all, the role of a franchisee is to run a business and that takes a different mindset to the day-to-day workings of a physiotherapist. We now have two franchisees without clinical experience and another partnership where one is a physio and one isn't. Basically, it comes down to whether the person is the right fit. Physio experience can obviously be an advantage, but there's lots more to it than that.

What services does Active+ offer?
As we've grown, our vision has shifted from being the leading brand of physiotherapy to now aiming to be the leading brand of integrated allied health clinicians. We are one of only a few physio-based practices that have gone in that direction so comprehensively in New Zealand. Our recent branding has talked about this important connection between mind and body.

All sorts of multidisciplinary inputs are required to help you function holistically. For example, you might come and see us because you've sprained your ankle while training for that marathon, but you're also talking about your headaches. So it might be that you're not breathing correctly or that you're just a real stress cadet. We can offer the total solution, not just working on your ankle. In this example, you may want to talk to one of our psychologists about reducing your stress levels or a pain specialist doctor about what triggers your headaches.

Specifically, Active+ offers:

- Physiotherapy
- Pilates
- Gym
- Occupational Therapy
- Psychology and Counselling
- Dietitians and Nutritionists
- Vocational Counsellors
- Social Workers and Social Support
- Medical Specialists

How do clients benefit from using a franchised physiotherapist?
Physio practices need to comply with a myriad of government legislation and that involves lots of work and expense. This includes things like health and safety and the Privacy Act. When people look for a physio practice, most trust that all these requirements are in place, but they may not be. Active+ has the added credibility here because we built our entire system around quality standards and government compliance. I was involved in the actual design of these in the 1990s. That means that every new franchise is automatically accredited to the systems by external auditing bodies.

We also see this credibility extend by word of mouth between locations. For example, if someone has a good experience with our Whanganui franchise, they may refer someone to our Dominion Road practice or visit it themselves if they are in the area. This consistency of service is another major benefit of using a franchise. It doesn't matter which of our locations you choose, the service will be of an equally high standard. This removes any risk for clients.

What problems have you run into as the franchise has grown?
Sometimes life has got in the way for our franchisees. I think it can be difficult for parents of young children simply because of the time constraints. Looking after small children, running a home and nurturing a business at the same time can be a big ask. Not impossible by any means, but certainly a challenge.

In many ways, the business is like a child as well. You can't ignore it or walk away from it and pick it up in three years-time or so when you've got more time. So we have had cases where our franchisee has elected to sell or leave because of their family commitments.

We have also had franchisees leave because they didn't like our interdisciplinary environment. They would rather remain as physiotherapists only and not offer the total solution. The great thing about those who have left is the amicable way it's happened. It's important that the franchisor–franchisee relationship works well for both parties and if it doesn't, we need to work through it. We've never had to go to court over this and, in fact, some of our ex-franchisees are very supportive of what we are doing.

What are your aims for the next ten years?
Our big focus is to grow our brand into other regions of New Zealand and remain 100 percent New Zealand owned and operated. Over the last few years there has been enormous overseas investment into New Zealand rehabilitation companies, which seems extraordinary because margins are extremely tight in the delivery of

quality services. We believe that Kiwis would value at the very least a choice of having access to New Zealand owned and operated rehab services. We bring the following benefits as a uniquely Kiwi company:

- We are not under pressure to make returns to foreign investors who have major expectations around the value of the return
- The guiding principles of the company reflect our obligations under the Treaty of Waitangi
- We are committed to kaupapa Maori models which in essence are services delivered by Maori for Maori. So while we work in partnership with Maori Health Providers presently, we do so understanding that eventually our Maori partners will be enabled and resourced to deliver services independently of us.

What advice would you give someone considering an Active+ franchise?

There are so many things to consider, but the big one is to look at what other life decisions they will make in the near future. I mentioned earlier how life has got in the way for some. Many make life decisions such as starting a family without factoring in how that will impact on the business. You can't make a life decision or a family decision without you and your partner considering the impact of that decision on the business because the business is like one of your children. It would be really nice for them if you could make a decision and the business just carries on. That may be possible in some franchise systems such as making yogurt or something, but not in physiotherapy because we deal with people. It's vital that we find the right people and franchising is right for them. That's why we have these hard conversations from the outset. Otherwise it can be a painful experience for everyone. We certainly want to grow our number of franchisees, but we only want people who tick all the boxes and have really thought it through.

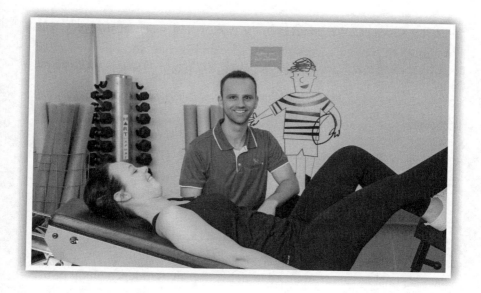

What are the core values of Active+?

The values we live by are the cornerstone of the entire franchise. The best piece of business advice I ever received was to know your values and uphold them in everything you do. We refer to our values whenever we make decisions. This ranges from buying equipment to interviewing potential franchisees. Our values are respect for all people, productivity and partnerships, resilience, connectedness to our communities and truth and validity.

Can you tell us more about a few of these values?

Respect for all people: This is such an important value in New Zealand today, being a multicultural society. We've attracted people from different ethnic backgrounds and other countries at Active+. We're all New Zealanders and we're here to help everyone be well.

Productivity and partnerships: This is about acknowledging that the usual teacher-pupil type or franchisor–franchisee relationship won't stay that way all the time. It recognises that at various times, the people you engage with will teach you as much as you teach them, and that's how that relationship is. This is important in a business sense because I think the franchisees feel empowered to offer their ideas, their creativity and their thinking to us at the franchisor level as much as we do to them. I couldn't have led a company for 30 years with the same drive if it hadn't been for other people from time to time wanting to lead a project or bring a new idea to the table. So that's a value that's another win–win and highlights that we're all in this together.

Connectedness to the community: This is important because we are all community-based clinicians. We don't see you in a hospital and our franchisees can become really important faces in the community just as those physios in my netball team were when I was 16. They were people within the community who were known. The right franchisees buy into that because they want to be a face in their community, and they want to be on the school board. We recently saw a good example of this at a football match where the son of one of our franchisees was playing. All of the parents on one side of the ground had their Active+ umbrellas out in support of the local school team. This is the sort of partnership between franchisees and their communities that's really important. Our community sees us as a place where they can come and get what they need to live well and holistically.

What specifically can you offer franchisees?
The automatic accreditation that our franchisees get to all government standards is huge. It not only saves them from the time-consuming and expensive process of proving compliance, but our system allows them better access to government funding. This system also allows them to run a more diverse business than other physiotherapy clinics without reinventing the wheel or taking a decade to perfect.

What do you look for in franchisees?
The first thing is the need for them to share our values. They also need to be loyal to the brand, forward thinking, brave in the face of a challenge and aspirational.

What advice would you give someone who is thinking about franchising their business?
Franchising a business is not as easy as it looks. It's hard work and takes time to get right. It's also vital that you get the right franchisees on-board. Some people can be tempted to grow their network of franchisees without taking the time to make sure that person is a good fit. This needs lots of research and hard conversations. It's a lot easier and in everyone's best interests to do this first, rather than have to pick up the pieces later. But when you do get the right people, believe in them like you believe in yourself.

What about someone looking at buying into a franchise?
There are still some people out there who think that buying into a franchise is a way to make passive income. That couldn't be further from the truth. It's a tough job and requires hard work. But if you're happy with that, your values align with the franchise and you want to be part of something bigger than yourself, it's a fantastic and rewarding option.

PAUL JAMIESON
FRANCHISOR OF KELLY SPORTS AND KELLY CLUB

"Inspiring kids is the greatest job in the world."
(Paul Jamieson)

PAUL JAMIESON
FRANCHISOR OF KELLY SPORTS AND KELLY CLUB

Paul Jamieson risked everything in 2008 when he became the owner of Kelly Sports, a franchise that runs sport-focused programmes for children. Soon after this he launched Kelly Club, a similar business that offers formal before and after school care and holiday programme services.

Paul believes there are two main keys to being a successful franchisor. The first is an absolute dedication to making life easier for franchisees. The second is a commitment to making a real difference to the lives of the customers or clients that the franchise serves.

Paul has become a top New Zealand franchise leader by showing how effective these principles are. He has grown Kelly Sports from seven to 36 franchise zones and Kelly Club from zero to 68 franchisees over a relatively short period of time.

Paul is passionate about children and the work he does. That shines through in the following pages.

How did you first get involved with the franchise?

I bought the Auckland master franchise for Kelly Sports in 2008. That was a big decision because I had to uproot my family from Wellington. At the time I thought we could do something bigger with it and that's why I ended up buying the entire franchise in 2011. I've never looked back since.

Kelly Club wasn't around at that point. The idea came when I was looking for more opportunities for my franchisees and their coaches. While Kelly Sports was working well, the focus was mainly on running afterschool sessions for an hour or so a day. I thought we may also be able to deliver longer and more varied programmes as an afterschool care service. From my research I felt that a lot of what was currently being offered was a glorified babysitting service and we could provide something far better. So Kelly Club was born. It couldn't be called 'Kelly Sports Before and After School Care' because it would involve more than just sport. That's why we named it Kelly Club.

The two complement each other really well. Lots of our schools have both programmes. Kelly Sports after school sessions usually run from 3.10pm until 4.10pm, while Kelly Club continues until 6pm. A number of our franchisees offer both brands and the rest focus on just one.

Is the role of franchisor what you expected?

When I look back on the first business plan I created, it looks quite different now to what it did back at the beginning, but the role is pretty much what I expected. Even when I had the master franchise, the focus was always about how to make things better for our franchisees and that hasn't changed. It's sometimes been challenging, particularly around Kelly Club, because there's a lot of compliance and regulations that we need to adhere to and this takes up time for us nationally and at the local level with the franchisees.

The feedback we get from parents, kids and teachers makes it all worthwhile. It shows us what a difference we make to kids' lives. That was the thing that hit home the most. I've always been child-centric and I've always loved sport but to really see the difference that we're making is priceless. When our staff walk into a school, they're superstars to the kids.

What's the biggest sacrifice you've had to make?

I put everything on the line to do this. We sold our family home, sold other rental property and literally invested our entire life and livelihood in it. I had a good corporate job in Wellington and a great lifestyle but risked all of that to do something I believed in and something I was passionate about.

What big risks do you face?

The single biggest risk is that we're dealing with people's most precious cargo in their children. There's no one more important in a parent's life than their child and we're charged with looking after thousands of them up and down the country every day.

That's never far from my mind and it's why we've got strict systems and processes in place around health and safety and compliance.

What has changed over 12 years?

There's a lot more compliance as I've already mentioned, particularly for Kelly Club. That means more work for the franchisees rather than just being able to get out there and create awesome, fun opportunities for kids. But parents and kids haven't seen much of a change because we make sure all those things are managed in the background.

(Paul talks with kids at a Kelly Sports programme)

How well has the business grown?

When I started, we had a little desk at home and it was just my wife and I, but now we have a head office team of 15. Kelly Sports has grown from seven franchise zones to 36, while Kelly Club has gone from zero to 68. The growth isn't something I reflect on very often until people remind me. I think that's because I'm always looking for those next milestones and reaching our overarching mission of being in communities throughout New Zealand. We're in lots of communities but there are others we haven't got to yet. We're told every day how much of an impact we're having and I'm passionate about doing more and reaching more areas.

What qualities do you look for in potential franchisees?

I feel I'm well qualified to find franchisees because I've been one. I understood what their challenges are and what's needed to succeed. Being of good character and transparent are important attributes to me. That's how I approach life personally and from a business perspective. That way you don't need to wonder what you've said to anybody. You just need to remember what the truth is and what actually happened. Not everyone follows that approach, but for me, it's the only way to succeed in anything.

Another big quality for me is passion. It's a word that a lot of people use to describe me. They always tell me they love my passion and enthusiasm and that's because I am that way. I really believe in what we're doing and I need franchisees to feel the same. If I was just interested in the business of making money, I'd probably do something less complicated and with less work. But at the end of the day I'm passionate about kids, I'm passionate about making a difference and that's what inspires me. My proudest moments are when I walk into any of our programmes and see kids having a great time. Knowing that I've played a part in making that happen really spins my wheels. That's what I want our franchisees to feel.

Anybody in business also needs to be personable and be able to relate to people. I look for this as well as people who are good listeners. In business you have to listen. We have to listen to our customers, our funders, our schools and most importantly the children who attend our programmes. People who aren't good listeners wouldn't succeed in this business.

What marketing do you do?

The majority of our business comes from or is based at schools so the marketing we do is mainly focused on the schools. We do a lot of direct communication aimed at parents like contributing to school newsletters, sending flyers home with kids or in digital formats. All of our individual clubs or sport franchise zones also have their own Facebook pages. We find that focused marketing is far more successful. Even community newspapers aren't getting to our core targets like direct marketing does.

We also go into other schools to showcase our programmes with free clinics. Our marketing of both brands complement each other well. For example, if a Kelly Sports franchisee goes into a school within a zone to showcase programmes, Kelly Club is likely to be part of that conversation and vice versa.

What myths are there around franchising?
I think there's a myth that it's only the franchisor that gets anything out of a franchise system. There may be some franchises that ask you to sign a piece of paper, pay them money and give them a phone number to ring if they have a problem. But that's not how most work. A good system is about wanting everyone to make money. That's not only the right thing to do, but its good business because if the franchisee makes money, the franchisor makes money.

What support do you give your franchisees?
We give them comprehensive support initially with their induction, but also ongoing so that it's almost a turn-key operation with both Kelly Club and Kelly Sports. Our dedicated relationship managers help them through the entire process. We support them all the way from supplying their equipment through to helping build their initial sales. We also spend time formulating their business plan because every zone and school is different and everyone has different skills and needs support in different areas. I'm a great believer that if you don't know where you're going, any road will get you there. So having a good plan and then helping our franchisees get to their target destination is critical for everyone.

(Paul chats with a franchisee)

Would you do anything differently if you could start again?

I'd probably look to empower the franchisees more so they could be more self-sufficient. I've been wanting to help so much and minimise things going wrong to the point where I may have gone too far at times. You never want something serious to go wrong but sometimes those little learning outcomes are important when things don't always go your way. In sporting terms, it's like saying you sometimes learn more from a loss than a win.

How is Kelly Group different from more traditional franchises?

I mentioned earlier how important communication skills are for myself and franchisees. I think that's more important for this niche than most others. The nature of the business, particularly with Kelly Sports, means we need to be more proactive and we need to chase our opportunities.

If you're a Subway or a McDonald's and set up in the right location, you're almost guaranteed to succeed. People know who you are, where you are and exactly what you offer. We've got a great story and a great reputation but we need to work harder to make sure people are fully aware of who we are and what we do.

Some of our people don't necessarily have the confidence to go banging on doors and have those conversations. This can be intimidating stuff. For example, we have to meet school principals. Some of our guys might've only been to the principal's office when they were sent there to be told off when they attended school all those years ago, and now they've got to go in there and sell them something or talk to them about what we can do. That's why we spend quite a bit of time on sales training.

What advice would you give someone looking at franchising their business?

The first thing you need to realise is that not every business is franchisable, and if yours is, do you want to go down that route? It's natural that lots of people think they've got something good they can replicate and make successful, but there are lots of things to consider. For example, if the business's intellectual property is too much about the individual person, it's difficult to make it work because that can be difficult to transfer to franchisees.

This can also be a problem in reverse. Let me explain. I've had some pretty well known people wanting to come on board with me. Having their names associated with the business would be fantastic, but that's not what it's about. I need passionate people who are focused on Kelly Sports or Kelly Club, not their own brands. If I had a high profile person as a franchisee, he or she may be more concerned about his or her own brand, or parents might be attracted to the business because of that person's reputation. It's important that the focus is on what we do and our brand first and foremost. That's not to say a high-profile person wouldn't work, but it's important that the business is the focus and not any one individual.

I think you need a genuine reason to franchise a business and not just to make money. It's a hard slog so you need to be in it for the right reasons and be driven by them. For me it was easy because I'm passionate about kids, sport and making a difference. We make a difference in the lives of our franchisees, their staff, as well as the parents of the kids who attend our programmes. After all, most parents don't choose to go to work, but they need to pay the bills and need to know their kids are in a happy, safe and caring environment.

(A Kelly Sports video)

We also make a massive difference to the lives of the kids who attend our programmes. One of the things I love the most is seeing kids annoyed when mum or dad come to pick them up early. That may sound strange but it's because they think they're going to miss out on an activity or playing a game. That just shows me how much they enjoy being at our programme and I know the parents are happy that their kids are having a great time. So before franchising, people need to ask themselves, "Who will this make a difference for?"

One thing some people don't give enough attention to is the importance of adding value to their franchisees. I had some people visit recently about franchising their business. They currently had someone working for them who was more of a franchisee than an employee. I asked them what support they gave him. Their response was that he didn't need much help from them so they just let him please himself under their brand. That's a fateful mistake for any franchisor because your franchisees will always want to know what they're paying for and what value you are adding to their business.

Failure to continually support a franchisee can lead to all sorts of problems. It can affect your reputation through word of mouth spreading and it can also reach social and traditional media. This has happened to a few big franchises in Australia recently. So it's important to be aware of how different a franchisor-franchisee relationship is from a standard employer-employee arrangement.

You need to be able to sign a franchise agreement, put it in a bottom drawer and only bring it out when someone wants to sell or move on. If we need to pull an agreement out sooner than that, I know something's wrong because it means we're not hitting the milestones that either one of us wanted.

There are also other risks and things that can go wrong for franchisors. That's why it's vital to be in the game for the right reasons. Otherwise it will all seem too hard and be unlikely to last. But if the passion and reasons are there, it's a hugely rewarding thing to do.

SIMON HARKNESS
CEO OF KITCHEN STUDIO

"Even in such technical lines as engineering, about 15 percent of one's financial success is due to one's technical knowledge and about 85 percent is due to skill in personal engineering, to personality and the ability to lead people."
(Dale Carnegie)

SIMON HARKNESS
CEO OF KITCHEN STUDIO

Simon Harkness has been in retail senior management since 2001. The first six years were spent in corporate roles, while the remainder have been in the franchise sector. This combination of corporate and franchise experience at a senior management level has helped him become a top New Zealand franchise leader.

His role as a franchise leader differs a bit from others in this book because Kitchen Studio is a cooperative. This creates its own unique challenges, while many of the issues he faces on a day-to-day basis are similar to his more traditional franchise counterparts.

Since Simon joined the company, turnover and the share value has significantly increased and Kitchen Studio has been voted the country's most trusted kitchen brand for three straight years.

The most trusted kitchen brand in New Zealand

How does the cooperative model differ from standard franchises?
The big difference is that we are owned by the franchisees and all the profits and dividends go directly back to them. This means the franchisees have more power and the franchisor can't dictate in the same way as he or she might in the more traditional franchise model. The culture is more inclusive and consultative and franchisees are represented around the board table and have a say in the strategic direction of the business. That said, we do have to make decisions in the best interests of the business which at times may not be popular, but we generally work with the network so that this becomes an inclusive decision.

Since moving into the franchise sector in 2006, what trends have you noticed?
There are now a lot more franchises in all sectors. That means there's more competition for franchisees and greater expectation from customers. I've also noticed a growing demand for quality service and that's something we take extremely seriously. More customers also like to know they are dealing with the business owner these days rather than employees. This puts franchising in a strong position when franchisees can take the lead in this area as we do at Kitchen Studio.

How does a franchise CEO role differ from a non-franchise CEO?
Corporate leadership and franchise leadership are quite different. It's important to understand each so a franchise CEO can incorporate the best of both. There's more of a human factor in franchising, having a collaborative relationship with franchisees and trusting them to run their business in accordance with the system. This is quite different from the standard employer–employee model where one has total dominance over the other. The collaborative focus with franchising is even more obvious in a cooperative like Kitchen Studio.

What services does Kitchen Studio offer?

First and foremost, we listen to what our clients want and are looking for in their dream kitchen. We help the clients create a kitchen design that works for them, their lifestyle and their home. We then build it, install it and back it up with a double trust guarantee. This includes the deposit being held in trust so it's security is guaranteed, while the ten-year guarantee for the kitchen is transferable to new owners if the house is sold within that timeframe.

How does Kitchen Studio differ from other kitchen suppliers?

One thing our clients tell us all the time is that we are far more attentive and truly listen to them. This is a key focus of our design network and a huge part of the service we offer. Successful designers listen. It's as simple as that. Designing and building a new kitchen is a big investment for clients and it's important it's exactly as the customer wants it. It's not like buying a car where if you don't like it you can just go out and buy another one. It's usually a 20-year investment.

What's your biggest highlight during your time with Kitchen Studio?

Probably the massive growth in turnover the franchise has had. We've forged strong partnerships with our approved suppliers and created a platform to help us grow our network. This has needed our focus and I'm pleased to say we're now very excited about the future. This is also underpinned by us launching a new business system that allows us to add greater efficiency and speed from the design to the installation.

Tell us about this year's Trusted Brand award?

Kiwis have voted us New Zealand's most trusted kitchen designers and manufacturers for three years in a row now. This is another highlight for me and a huge honour for everyone in the company. It identifies us as a brand that customers believe in and trust with the extremely intricate task of designing and delivering their dream kitchen.

There are many benefits to winning these awards. Firstly, it puts us in illustrious company alongside iconic companies like Air New Zealand, Fisher & Paykel and Toyota. It also creates a great sense of pride among people in the franchise and pushes them to work even harder to keep delivering on the trust promise so that Kitchen Studio is well placed to keep winning this award.

What is the most misunderstood facet of franchising?

I've had a sense that some people think a franchisor will guarantee a positive outcome when it is the franchisees that must deliver success. Then when the franchisee doesn't do the work and fails to achieve the expected results, he or she blames the franchisor for not providing enough support. I think sometimes franchisees are given this impression that they can't fail, but some also just expect the results to come. As a cooperative, we're a bit different because we're working for the whole network and the profits go back to the franchisees.

I also think some people don't appreciate the differences between franchises and corporates. For example, if a corporate had a number of stores working and others failing, they may decide to increase funding to those underperforming stores to bring them up to the level of the others. They could also close those that weren't making a healthy profit. As a franchise, and even more so for a cooperative, we can't do that. Everyone has to be treated the same. So we have to focus on maximising the returns for each franchise individually. This illustrates one major difference between franchises and corporates.

What future plans do you have for Kitchen Studio?
We intend to expand into territories we haven't been before and increase our footprint in existing areas. I'm a huge fan of training and supporting our franchisees. This is one of the most important parts of the role of a franchise CEO. We've already increased this significantly since I came on board. We have a dedicated Franchise Development Manager who delivers strategy sessions and business support to each franchisee. It's important to remember that not all franchisees are experienced business managers, even those who have come from their own businesses or roles in others.

I'm dedicated to ongoing training, not one-off events. This has been important to me for many years after a colleague posed a question to me. He said, "Do you think Roger Federer stopped training once he won the US Open or Tiger Woods stopped training after he won his first US Masters?" I think we all know the answer to those questions and it should be the same in franchising.

I'm also excited about our new business system. This will allow us to deliver the many processes involved in the design, quote, order, manufacture and installation of a kitchen as one seamless project. This will make things far easier for franchisees and clients. We've managed to streamline everything and bring it all together in the one system.

What marketing do you do?

We're focused on a mixture of marketing channels, both online and offline. Customers love to see images of our work, particularly examples from their regions. This is shown through our website and our showrooms from Dunedin to Auckland. Our website video testimonials are also highly effective in attracting customers. These are important because, as I mentioned earlier, our success all comes down to trust and there's no-one better to highlight that than our happy clients. Google reviews are another example of this, as is word of mouth.

(A Kitchen Studio design)

Sometimes the marketing channel we use will come down to what's most effective for the message we want to communicate. For example, if the message is purely one of trust, bus and taxi advertising are great options. We also use traditional media, but at this stage we have moved away from television because we get better value for money in other media streams. We were pleased to have our marketing recognised last year by winning runner-up at the Trusted Brands Marketing Awards.

Our marketing is usually focused on a specific promotion, such as offering high quality upgrades and discounts for free. These promotions are available nationally at all of our 15 showrooms and home shows and kitchen expos across New Zealand. These offers are very well supported by our approved local and global suppliers.

Have you had any mentors along your career journey?
I'm fortunate to have had some good, grounded people in my life who have offered great advice when I've asked for it and sometimes when I haven't. Having worked across a number of national retail business in different disciplines, this has given me a strong understanding of business and how people make it all work. One person I've always had great respect for is Stephen Tindal. I worked for him when I started in retail. He's a great example of how we should conduct ourselves in business.

What advice would you have for someone who is looking at investing in a franchise?
It's important to take your time before buying into a franchise. There are three important things to do when you start your search. Firstly, look for a business with strong values, but don't just find out what those values

are. Look for examples of those being lived across that group. It's one thing to list values on a website, but quite another to live by them.

Secondly, talk to franchisees in that network and ask them what does and doesn't work for them in belonging to that franchise group. And thirdly, it's vital to seek independent advice from someone you trust.

What do you do to keep motivated and healthy?

The old cliché that the role of CEO is the loneliest job in the world depends on how many good people you have around you to act as sounding boards and encourage you to forge ahead with good ideas. In this regard I'm lucky to have a great team around me. Since joining Kitchen Studio, it's been a very busy time, relocating our Support Office from Christchurch to Auckland and growing the business to where it is today, strong both financially and culturally. When I do have a break I love to spend time with family and friends, go fishing and play golf.

What qualities do you look for in franchisees?

Having all-round good business acumen is always important but they must be good people who are genuinely invested in succeeding within a group of likeminded people. A franchisee needs a positive can-do attitude and must be willing to work within a franchise framework. There are always people who want to change the system because they think they have a better idea but these particular people will always struggle to be successful in a franchise model. A potential franchisee must also have a good financial platform so they start off on the right foot and a personal support network to help them through the good and not so good times.

(Another Kitchen Studio design)

What support do you offer your franchisees?

We have a network of knowledgeable business people and franchisees who have many years of experience at Kitchen Studio. This support is invaluable in helping new franchisees understand the system and the Kitchen Studio Way. We're also planning on developing The Kitchen Studio Academy, an online portal that has a knowledge base and offers training and support for existing and new franchise owners.

What does success mean to you and how do you achieve it?

If a franchise system is sustainable and the individual franchisees are able to create value on the way through and then are able to sell for a profit and there is still more opportunity for the new franchisee and franchisor, then we've succeeded in our mission.

What risks does the franchise have and how do you manage those?
Being a business owner is always a risk, but by being in our network, we are able to guide and support franchisees with sound business systems. We have a board with elected shareholder directors and independent directors responsible for the governance of the business. They have a sound understanding of the existing business and are influential in the strategic direction of the group. This ultimately helps improve the health of Kitchen Studio and reduce the risks for the franchisee and the franchisor.

What do you like most about your role?
Always trying to help our franchisees and making the whole Kitchen Studio business a success. Every day is different and we're part of a great group of people who make up our network.

I'm also lucky to work with such a dedicated team in our Support Office who are all focused on maintaining the core business for the shareholders and helping and supporting the franchisees and their teams to be the best that they can be.

Our success is a lot about what the franchisees achieve. They appreciate that the team at our Support Office are dedicated and passionate about helping them be successful in their individual businesses and ultimately driving the success of the Kitchen Studio Group.

How do you see the future of franchising in NZ?
The franchise model is very strong in New Zealand, growing hugely in the last ten years. I see this continuing to be the case over the next decade because it realises the dream of so many New Zealanders who want to own their own businesses. For many it allows them to be in business for themselves, but not by themselves.

SIMON MCKEARNEY
EXECUTIVE GENERAL MANAGER
OF HELLOWORLD NEW ZEALAND

*"Always let your courage
be greater than your fears."*
(Unknown)

SIMON MCKEARNEY
EXECUTIVE GENERAL MANAGER OF HELLOWORLD NEW ZEALAND

Simon McKearney, along with a talented management team, has taken Helloworld New Zealand from nowhere to a billion-dollar plus franchise in just over three years. This makes him not only a clear industry leader in the travel sector, but one of New Zealand's top franchise leaders.

He faced huge challenges when he moved from Flight Centre to Helloworld in 2016. Many of the franchisees were in dire trouble and struggling to make ends meet.

Fast-forward three years and most of the now 70-plus franchisees are thriving thanks to the massive growth in the value proposition that focuses on support as well as monumental changes to the company strategy. This culminated last year with Helloworld winning one of the most prestigious travel industry awards – Top Retail Travel Brand.

Tell us about your background before Helloworld.

Helloworld New Zealand was launched in February 2016. I joined a few months before that to literally kick start the brand here in New Zealand. Going back in history, I was with Flight Centre for nine years, which was, and still is, a major player in the travel marketplace. I began my career there as the CFO, where I worked with every division of the company. This in turn taught me the different aspects of the travel business, especially seeing how the front-end travel agent needed to operate effectively for continued success.

I left Flight Centre and two days after that I walked into Helloworld. In the first part of this journey was the task of bringing together Harvey World Travel, Air New Zealand Holidays and United Travel into a single brand. It had always proven to be a difficult task to get Helloworld up and running as the franchise networks in New Zealand had always competed against each other and didn't want to relent and give up their own respective brand names. I had an easier perspective on this as I had not been involved in any of the past and I had been brought on to do a job that needed to be done as quickly as possible.

Helloworld in Australia had been going five years before the launch in New Zealand. They had spent considerable amounts of money bringing different brands under the Helloworld umbrella, yet they'd never been able to get strong consumer cut through in terms of brand recognition. This was something we were determined to get right in the launch into our market.

What early challenges did you face?

It was a tough job made easier with the support of some real 'believers' in what needed to be achieved. It wasn't a case of just walking in there and starting a brand. A culture of support from a head office point of view needed to be created in conjunction with the delivery of the external brand.

I pretty much announced to everyone when I came in that we would launch in eight weeks. That would get us through our Christmas period and into the New Year and basically kick it to life at the beginning of February. I really plucked that time out of thin air but eight weeks sounded about right for the marketing team to get messaging organised along with the plans they had previously laid. It would also give us time to 'paint our stores blue'.

This led to a funny story because one of the younger members of the marketing team approached me to say that eight weeks wouldn't work. I told her that if we all worked together, we could do it. I realised she had been brave enough to front the new EGM so I wanted to encourage belief that working together could achieve great things. She was so sure the date wouldn't work as she calmly explained that if we insisted on this date, the launch date would fall on Waitangi Day and none of our stores would actually be open that day. The first big decision I made could have ended in disaster, but thankfully her courage to let us know saved that from happening.

In the end, we delayed it a week, which meant that our grand launch would happen on Valentine's Day. So our anniversary now is on Valentine's Day and we joke internally that you can now give the flowers and travel brochures on the same day.

There were lots of challenges to deal with in those early days. The owners of the long-established United Travel stores who were a very tight group in their own right, started to leave the business because they didn't want to face the reality of having to change their name. They served notice and announced that their entire network was going to leave and form their own brand, which they did. So, I walked into a bit of a mess regarding that particular event. One minor point they had overlooked was that they didn't own the name United Travel so had to start again anyway. It seems crazy how such simple things can ruin age-old businesses.

As a positive, we had quite a few Harvey World Travel stores that had agreed to come over to be Helloworld, but these numbers in this brand were declining steadily year on year. In the end, we convinced about 43 members to rebrand and become what we now know as the Helloworld Travel brand. That was our starting point. Thankfully, the business is in far better shape now with 70-plus stores across New Zealand and growing rapidly, along with a huge number of independent travel agents who have also joined but remain as their own specific business name.

(Inside the central Auckland Helloworld store)

What support do your franchisees get?

I guess anyone in a collective network, regardless of industry, can call themselves a 'franchise network', even if it's because they just have an agreement. But to me, that doesn't make it a real franchise network. We were kidding ourselves in those early days regarding what we offered the network and we were never meeting the expectation of what true franchising means.

What we did set about doing when I came on board was to go to the members and ask them what they needed to make their businesses not only successful but also sustainable. We also asked what they could pay for given the respective margins and profitability they had. We then set about creating the new value proposition.

The first thing they wanted was 'best in industry' national marketing, which is a big deal if you want to get your brand out there, competing head to head with others. We've got a great marketing team here that will take the message from buyers, add our flavour to it and take it to market every single day through our various marketing channels.

Also high on the list of wants was comprehensive and differentiated products to take to the marketplace. We now have a major in-house product supplier under the name of GO wholesale who don't have a peer in the market. We can create exclusive deals through our own channels as well as provide a massive array of travel products across the globe at prices that lead the market.

In terms of connecting the members, we have a couple of large conferences for franchisees each year that offer a smorgasbord of learning, inspiration and entertainment. We also have regional meetings for more regular updates and we speak individually to franchisees in their own stores at least every quarter.

Comprehensive training is a big part of our support. This isn't just learning about individual products, but also training in leadership, human resources and business management. It all depends on where individual stores need support. For example, a store might be great at selling travel products, but they might not be experts at the day-to-day running of the business. So we'll go in and deliver help in that space.

Support in the area of technology is important because travel is an industry where technology is forever evolving. This isn't just for booking tools, but itinerary tools, local marketing tools, KPI tracking and many other areas of the business. We provide a lot of this technology which we in turn source from our global parent. This makes it very cost-effective.

We also help franchisees prepare their stores for opening. This includes quite a large financial contribution in the form of signage, fit-out guidance and painting to brand standard. We believe this is extremely good value.

Within the marketing team, those focused on national marketing work across digital and the various social media platforms. Traditional press and television advertising is another area looked after at head office. This is all about getting the messaging of our products out to the marketplace.

We also have staff dedicated to local store marketing. It's important that we support franchisees to get out into their communities and this is the focus of these staff. For example, if a franchisee is supporting a local fundraiser, the marketing staff may create brochures or other material for them. This could also be in the form of a local expo they're running.

All these deliverables add up to what we call the Helloworld Value Proposition. We charge a nominal franchise fee for all of this. There certainly isn't anything close to it in the travel industry that provides so much for such a little cost.

Tell us about the recent awards you've won?
We were judged the Best Travel Brand at last year's National Travel Industry Association awards in just our third year of operation. A major competitor had consistently won, so it was a great achievement for us at such an early stage of the franchise. Our growth has been truly remarkable since our early days when 43 stores comprised the brand. This is a result of pure determination by fantastic head office staff committed to delivering world class support, combined with franchisees who believed in what we were trying to achieve and held on tight for the ride.

Some of them had been really struggling over the years, mainly because the support wasn't there for them previously. But most of them have now turned things around and are now highly successful. There are so many stories of members who were down to one or two consultants sitting in a store and losing money who now have over a dozen employees in their stores making significant profits. That was all part of our story that we shared at the industry awards. We won the award on the back of that growth. That growth has continued this year. The profitability of our franchisees has improved again and they're employing even more people.

We were also voted the ninth best place to work this year in the Canstar awards. These are quite prestigious awards that are voted on by the marketplace, not employees. This was another huge honour, particularly since it covered all industries, not just travel.

Finally, our marketing team has had some phenomenal success and recognition which is just reward for the work they have been delivering.

What's your biggest highlight so far?
The awards were big, but they're really a consequence of what we've done as one large collection of amazing people. We're now a billion-dollar company four years after we were kicked in to life when we weren't quite sure how this was all going to pan out.

I have the privilege of telling this story in numerous settings and presentations as it's a fantastic New Zealand business story. But I always acknowledge that I'm speaking on behalf of everyone at Helloworld, because it's certainly not all about me. I just happen to be the leader. It's all the people who have come on board and contributed immensely and believed in what we could do. We were certainly struggling against the likes of Flight Centre and House of Travel given what they had achieved over a long period of time. We were just a distant third, if you could even say there were three in the game. But now we're head to head with these much larger established 40-year-old companies and can certainly foot it evenly in terms of what we offer.

Is leading a franchise what you expected?
Lots of people said to me before coming here that it's easier to control and drive behaviour when leading a wholly-owned company like Flight

Centre. At Flight Centre we could basically tell people what to do and as they were employees they were obligated to do it. But in a franchise like Helloworld, you don't have that power and you're held to account more by the franchisees and that's understandable. It's their livelihood that you look after and they've put their own money into their business. They need to run it profitably to pay the mortgage and buy the groceries. So their accountability is a lot higher and our responsibilities are higher, but on the flip side, the reward of seeing their success is greater. So was it what I expected? I learned a lot in terms of that accountability and delivering, which is something we all take extremely seriously in the management team here.

You mentioned marketing earlier. Is there any marketing you do that's unique to Helloworld?
We do lots of data analysis and we've found that New Zealand travellers really are creatures of habit. They go to the same places at the same times. So when you map all that out you realise that places like Sri Lanka, Tahiti and the Maldives are aspirational destinations, but only a very small percentages of New Zealanders go there. Fifty percent of travellers go to Australia and 25 percent visit the Pacific Islands. Then you add in Europe at a certain time of the year and the US and you've pretty much covered everywhere New Zealanders travel.

From this data we've created a 'supply chain team' that knows exactly what the customer is looking for in any given week. So we have the year pretty much mapped out and know exactly when to market Australia, Fiji and the other destinations New Zealanders want to travel to. This means that if a supplier comes to us wanting to advertise a particular destination in a particular week, we can tell them whether it's the best time or whether to wait for a better time to make a better return. I believe we are the only company in the industry using this supply chain concept.

(Some of the marketing and retail team on Pink Ribbon Day)

Do you think there are any misconceptions out there about franchising?

The misconception would be that it's a guaranteed good income. I think some people are happy to invest their money in a franchise because they think it can't fail. You still have to work hard. You've also got to be collaborative and work with the franchisor in a two-way relationship. If this is done and the system is followed, it can be a highly profitable and rewarding way of life.

What do you look for in franchisees?

Proven business performance is helpful but an attitude to want to succeed and want to believe is the most important attribute. We also want team players because it's a competitive industry and that competition doesn't just come from travel agents but numerous online competitors.

What advice would you give someone wanting to invest in a franchise?

There's the old adage about chasing something you're passionate about. But I think you can be passionate about most things. You want to evaluate to make sure you can see yourself lasting and adding value to your franchise business as well as the franchise network. You don't want to let emotion get in the way of good decisions. So I think passion shouldn't necessarily be first and foremost. I think interest is a better way to view it. You can have hobbies outside your working career and follow your passion that way. For example, you might have a passion about helping reduce child poverty but you don't have to go into business to do that. You can run a successful business in a different niche and help with child poverty either in your spare time, donate money or develop some sort of sponsorship in that area.

What's the best piece of advice you've ever had?

Roadblocks will always appear as you create your journey. If you believe in something and have the determination to see it through, the roadblocks will be passed. Keep looking for ways around, which may not be the most obvious solution to start with. Just never give up because eventually it'll work out. That's advice I've been given throughout my career.

Another great piece of advice is the importance of bringing people on board to deal with areas you may not be an expert in. I have such clever people on my team who deal with things I have no in-depth technical knowledge of. You don't need to know everything if you hire people who are experts in their fields. That's a big reason for our success.

Do you have a business mentor you look up to?

I guess as one works through their career you encounter examples of not only good leadership but also bad. I've certainly had a share of both but my focus has often been to look at what they did and seek the best parts but then also remain committed to what my personal beliefs are in order to have my own leadership 'brand'. Many leaders make the classic mistake of being so profit-focused at the expense of everything else and that's not how the modern world works. My view is that you have to create the culture of your workplace first and foremost, then your employees and/or franchisees will believe in the business and deliver upon the vision and strategy.

NEXT STEPS IN FRANCHISING
BY SIMON LORD – FOUNDER, FRANCHISE NEW ZEALAND MEDIA

Simon has over 35 years' experience in franchising, beginning in the UK. During three years with a quick printing franchise, he saw the chain grow from 30 to over 100 stores and realised the strength of franchising as a concept. He then became marketing manager of the Wimpy hamburger franchise, which operated over 400 fast food restaurants.

In 1992, Simon founded *Franchise New Zealand*, the country's only dedicated franchise magazine. Now a multi-media operation, *Franchise New Zealand* is read and relied upon by a huge proportion of New Zealand franchise buyers and professionals. For more, see www.Franchise.co.nz

Simon was a Board Member of the Franchise Association of New Zealand from its foundation in 1996 until 2007, and served as Chair from 2003-2005.

As the case studies in this book have shown, franchising is one of the most dynamic forms of marketing and distribution yet invented. By combining proven brands and systems with local capital and commitment, it offers a way for good companies to grow, and a way for small business owners to compete with the corporates on their doorstep.

If you've been inspired to learn more about franchising, what do you need to consider? Well, that rather depends on whether you want to:

- Franchise your own business;
- Take up a master franchise; or
- Become a franchisee yourself.

Franchise your own business

The first thing to understand about becoming a franchisor is that you need to have a profitable, successful and proven business to start with. You don't franchise an 'idea' – that's just selling a dream, and it's not fair or ethical to ask others to invest in something which doesn't have a solid base behind it.

Ideally, you should have at least two or three years of trading results which show that your business is profitable and trending in the right direction. Don't expect franchising your business to *make* you profitable. Franchising can increase your profitability and market share, can bring in additional capital investment and improve buying power, but if you're not profitable to start with, don't franchise until you are. Waiting will also give you a full picture of seasonal trends, and a trading and cash-flow history on which to base your franchised business model.

The exception to this general rule is where the product or service being franchised is required to grow fast in order to achieve a competitive advantage or market dominance. In this case, the developers behind the franchise need to have a great deal of relevant experience in their sector.

Building a sustainable franchise network will take a great deal of time, effort and money. Don't be tempted to take short cuts or use non-specialist advisors – franchising is complex and every business model is different. Here are some areas to consider:

Viable

When franchising your business, the first area to consider is the financial one. Franchising is not a source of instant income for the franchisor. It requires substantial investment during the set-up stage and, even once the first franchisees are coming on board, sufficient funds to provide for training and supporting them until they are generating enough revenue to fund the services you will need to provide. You therefore need good capital reserves and ongoing cash-flow to fund your franchise programme.

When analysing your potential for franchising, you have to be certain that there are sufficient returns in the business to make it worthwhile for all parties. You will need healthy gross profit margins that provide a worthwhile return on their investment for the franchisee while enabling them to pay royalties to fund the services provided by the franchisor – and a profit contribution for the franchisor too. This cannot be done by padding your prices to an uncompetitive level but must be achieved within the constraints of the marketplace.

Replicable

The second area to consider is whether your business is replicable – can it work in other areas and in other hands? You must have operating systems that are capable of being taught to complete strangers, possibly people with no experience in your industry. At the same time, there needs to be some element of intellectual property that makes your business unique or hard to copy. This means that, before franchising your business, you must have your systems well documented and your operating systems and processes properly protected legally.

Marketable

Third, you must have a marketable brand or image which franchisees will be prepared to pay for and proud to use. It should be instantly recognisable, work in all parts of the country (and possibly internationally), be unique rather than generic and have full name and trademark protection.

Sustainable

Fourth, you must be able to demonstrate a long-term and consistent level of demand for your product or service. Businesses based on short-term fads don't work as franchises (although franchises may well stock fashion items). You must also be able to guarantee consistency of supply of the products or services your franchisees will need without major cost fluctuations. This can be an issue particularly where products are imported.

Controllable

Finally, your business must be capable of being controlled while being operated by individual owners. This is partly a question of having the right training and systems in place to ensure that standards and payment regimes are properly established, developed and audited from the very beginning. However, it is also a matter of good management. Franchisors need to be leaders, communicators and motivators more than operators. Making the mental transition from running a business to running a franchise is often the most difficult process of all.

Take up a master franchise

Rather than developing a whole new franchise from scratch, another option is to take up a master franchise or master licence from an existing franchise. A master franchisee takes on some of the responsibilities for developing the franchise in a particular region or country. They recruit, train and support individual franchisees and, in some cases, may also set up their own operations. In return, they generally receive a proportion of each new franchisee's initial and ongoing fees.

Some master franchisees at national level may not sub-franchise at all, retaining ownership of all their own outlets, like Taco Bell and Wendy's, for example. Some, like The Coffee Club or Speedy Signs, have no company-owned outlets, focusing totally on supporting franchisees. And others may operate a mix of company-owned and franchised outlets, like Pizza Hut.

Global brand, local owner

A national master franchisee therefore needs to be more entrepreneurial and have the skills, resources and contacts to develop the franchise locally. The franchise brand and systems may already exist, but will need to be adjusted to meet local conditions, while differences in factors like wage costs, rents, competition and brand awareness mean that any overseas franchise model needs to be carefully analysed by local specialists to ensure the same five criteria above are met.

Overseas companies often have little understanding of the local market so wise buyers seek to reduce the risks as far as possible by carrying out their own thorough research into likely demand for the product or service, and confirming that the price asked and the number of outlets proposed by the franchisor is realistic.

Become a franchisee

As this book shows, good franchisors are committed and experienced businesspeople with a deep knowledge of how their system works and how to help others get the best out of it. That means that buying a franchise can be one of the best ways of getting into your own business. Having said that, no matter how good a reputation the franchise might have, it also needs to be a good match for your personality, your skills, your goals and your finances.

With over 600 different franchises currently available in New Zealand, here are some questions to help potential franchisees assess any opportunity.

- Is the business a good match for your skills and abilities? Will it require people skills, financial skills, leadership ability? Does it match your personality?

- Establishing any business takes hard work and, initially, long hours. Is your family supportive? Can the business provide the lifestyle you want?

- Can you afford to support yourself until the business is able to pay you a decent wage? Will it provide the income you want in the future?

- How long has the company been operating, and how long has it been franchising? If there are already successful franchisees, it suggests that the system works and your risk is therefore lower.

- Is there a long-term future for the business? Does the business demonstrate an ability to adapt to new trends? Who are the competition? What advantages does the franchise have over competitors?

- Is the franchise a known name in New Zealand which will attract customers for you?

- How does the franchisor make money? Is there a large initial franchise fee, an ongoing royalty fee which is fixed or based on turnover, or a mark-up on products sold to you by the franchisor? Beware large initial fees – franchisors who only make money from selling franchises may not be interested in you once you've bought your franchise.

- Do you have to buy products or services from the franchisor? If so, are these at the same or a better price than you could buy elsewhere? Buying power should offer a number of benefits to franchisees, such as better pricing, better terms and/or promotional support. In some franchises, the value of the discounts available offsets the cost of the franchise fees.

- What training will you receive initially? How long is it? What does it cover?

- What level of ongoing support can you expect? Will you have regular visits from a member of the franchisor's team? Does the franchise share benchmarking information between franchisees? Does somebody help you analyse your performance and suggest improvements?

- What figures can the franchisor produce to back up his claims? Are they based on fact? Are the sales levels realistic? Who is already achieving them – and can you talk to them? What are the total costs?

- And if you are looking at buying a business from an existing franchisee, make sure you get their figures for the last three years (if they have been trading that long). Ask a franchise-experienced accountant to review them – do they seem realistic? And ask the franchisor where they see potential for improvement in that location?

Get the right advice from the right people

Whether you are looking to franchise your business, take up a master franchise or buy a new or existing franchise outlet, you'll want to find out a lot more about the subject before you go any further.

Franchise New Zealand is an online resource dedicated to helping people find out more about franchising. It's a rich source of advice on franchising your business and buying a franchise, as well as covering franchise management, news and opportunities. The website at www. franchise.co.nz also includes a directory of franchises as well as franchise experienced advisors such as accountants, bankers, consultants, lawyers and other services.

Getting good professional advice is essential – but it's even more important that you get that advice from the right people. Franchising is a specialist area, and it's important to use specialists to help you.

In the case of accountants, bankers and lawyers, a franchise-experienced advisor will already have a great deal of knowledge of the franchises operating in your chosen sector. They can help set you up for success and help you avoid some of the pitfalls.

If you're franchising your own business, it's highly advisable to use a good franchise consultant. Accountants and lawyers may know a lot, but franchising a business requires a structured approach including feasibility studies, costing, determination of fees and territories, implementation planning and much, much more before you ask a lawyer to draw up a franchise agreement. It's an area where small differences in key areas can make or break a franchise business model. Using a consultant might seem costly but, believe me, getting it wrong will cost you much, much more time and money.

When you're choosing a consultant, do make sure you check what experience they have had. Ask for references and follow them up and, importantly, talk to people that they did work for three to five years ago. Are both the franchisors and their franchisees making a reasonable return on their investment? Anyone can produce a plan that looks good on paper, but it's only a few years down the track that you can see whether it really was good advice or not.

In summary, franchising is a great way to build a business, whether as a franchisor or franchisee. As the franchisors in this book will all tell you, though, if you want to create a sustainable business of your own then you need to make sure the foundations are strong. Take your time, do your research and choose your advisors carefully, and you could be following in the footsteps of some big franchising names.

ABOUT THE AUTHOR

PETE BURDON

Ever since childhood, Pete has been fascinated by how people communicate and how that gets interpreted. That's why his entire career has been dedicated to helping people get their messages across to the right people and heard in the way they intended.

Equipped with Masters Degrees in Journalism and Communication Management from universities in New Zealand and Australia, he started his working life as a daily newspaper reporter and then as a government press secretary.

Following these roles, it became obvious to Pete that one thing distinguished winners from losers in all fields – their reputation and brand authority.

From that point on, his sole focus has been helping people protect and grow their reputations so they can win more business and grow their profits. For some, this is learning how to become a bestselling author and for others it's how to master the news media to protect and grow their brands.

Pete says reputations have become harder to cement in the digital age because it's harder to stand out from the crowd. This is because everyone has an online megaphone to spread their message. He says the key is to do things that set you apart and that's the focus of his work.

For the last 20 years, he has advised and trained high profile politicians and the leaders of many well known brands. He also helps lesser known business owners and entrepreneurs grow their profits by becoming thought leaders in their niches. These include small and medium business owners, entrepreneurs, authors and speakers.

As a bestselling international author, thought leader, media trainer and wealth creator, Pete inspires, trains and advises people how to grow their reputations and bottom lines in the same way he has done himself.

CONTACTING OUR CONTRIBUTORS

You've now seen why these contributors are New Zealand's top franchise leaders. In addition to that they all have amazing opportunities available for the right people. If you would like to find out more about those, you can contact them directly.

Paul Jamieson – Kelly Sports and Kelly Club
Email: paul@kellysports.co.nz
Website: www.kellysports.co.nz www.kellyclub.co.nz
Facebook.com/KellySportsNewZealand/
Facebook.com/KellyClubNewZealand/

Gill Webb – Active+
Email: headoffice@activeplus.co.nz
Website: www.activeplus.co.nz
Facebook.com/ActivePlusNZ/
Twitter.com/ActivePlusNZ

Simon McKearney – Helloworld
Email: simon.mckearney@helloworld.co.nz
Website: www.helloworld.co.nz

Simon Harkness – Kitchen Studio

Email: simon@kitchenstudio.co.nz

Website: www.kitchenstudio.co.nz

Facebook.com/KitchenStudioNZ

Youtube.com/c/KitchenStudioNewZealand

Instagram.com/kitchenstudionz

Brendon Lawry – Liquorland

Email: brendonl@liquorland.co.nz

Website: liquorland.co.nz

Karen and David Dovey – Exceed

Email: Systems@exceed.co.nz

Website: www.exceed.co.nz

Facebook.com/exceedfranchising

Instagram: exceed.nz

Twitter.com/exceednz

Grant McLauchlan and Rene Mangnus – CrestClean

Email: franchises@crestclean.co.nz

Websites: www.crestclean.co.nz

www.crest.co.nz

Scott Jenyns – Aramex/Fastway Couriers
Email: scott@fastway.co.nz
Website: www.aramex.co.nz
Facebook.com/AramexNZ
LinkedIn: Scott Jenyns

Adam Parore – Small Business Accounting
Email: enquiries@sba.co.nz
Website: www.sba.co.nz
Facebook.com/SBA.SmallBusinessAccounting

Andrew and Denise Lane – Night 'n Day
Email: Andrew@nightnday.co.nz denise@nightnday.co.nz
Website: www.nightnday.co.nz

Paul Bull – Signature Homes
Email: paulbull@signature.co.nz
Website: www.signature.co.nz
Facebook.com/SignatureHomesNZ
Instagram: @signaturehomesnz

Melanie and Jack Harper – Driving Miss Daisy
Email: melanie@drivingmissdaisy.co.nz jack@drivingmissdaisy.co.nz
Website: www.drivingmissdaisy.co.nz
Facebook.com/DrivingMissDaisyNZ/

RECOMMENDED RESOURCES

Leaders in Franchise Law

Contact Mark Sherry
or Alan Prescott

T (03) 352 2293 F (03) 352 2274 E legal@harmans.co.nz
P PO Box 5496, Christchurch 8542
Central City 79-81 Cashel Street, Central City, Christchurch 8011
Papanui 485 Papanui Road, Papanui, Christchurch 8053
www.harmans.co.nz

Thinking of franchising your business?

Do it once, do it right.

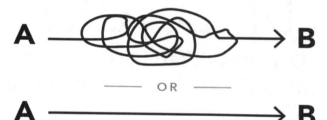

Talk first with New Zealand's largest, longest established and award winning team and get it right, first time.
Call Callum Floyd (09) 523 3858
or email callum@franchize.co.nz

New Zealand's Top Franchise Service Providers

www.franchise.co.nz

ADVICE
FREE MAGAZINE
DIRECTORY

Over 275 different franchises
+ specialist advisors and financiers

NEW ZEALAND'S
BEST SOURCE OF
FRANCHISING
INFORMATION
SINCE 1992

BUY YOUR OWN BUSINESS

Franchise
NEW ZEALAND

Want A Dynamic Speaker And Trainer At Your Next Conference?

Do your spokespeople know how to master media interviews in the digital age? Are you ready to communicate with journalists within minutes when a crisis strikes? Do your staff know what to do when approached by the media? When understood and mastered by everyone, knowledge in these areas goes a long way to cement reputations that are increasingly vulnerable in today's world.

PRESENTATION FORMATS

< Keynote

This engaging and thought-provoking programme will leave your conference or meeting participants with a new appreciation of the role of the news media, its requirements and how to create a mutually beneficial relationship with it.

Please allow 1 – 2 hours

< Full or Half Day Workshops

This is a 4 to 8 hour programme tailored to your individual organisation. This can focus entirely on the media interview process, crisis communication planning or a combination of these equally important areas. Includes workbooks and a crisis communication plan template for participants to take away.

< Staff Communication Training

These sessions show your staff how to communicate effectively in sales conversations, with angry people, persistent reporters and more formal presentations.

www.PeteBurdon.com

Extraordinary Products To Grow Those Media Skills And Get Your Crisis Communication Plan Underway

Bolstering those vital media skills can now be done in the comfort of your own living room. Explore our range of programmes focused on media interview training, crisis communication planning and other useful information. Cement your reputation now and give yourself the peace of mind by knowing you're ready for any media encounter, positive or negative.

Visit my website to view the full range of products

www.PeteBurdon.com

Discover How You Can Grow Your Business and Become The "Go To" Authority and Expert In Your Field

✔ Write a Book with Pete

✔ Get More Customers Using Pete's High Impact Direct Response Marketing

✔ Become an International Bestselling Author

To Find Out How, Visit:

www.StandoutBranding.com

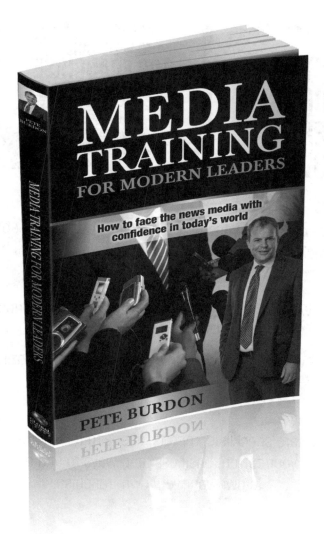

EXTRA BONUSES!!

EXTRA BONUSES HERE NOW!

We can't give you everything you need to know about franchising or growing your business in one small book.

So we've created a very special website with loads of extra **FREE** resources, just for you.

You'll find easy ways to get access to the amazing people featured in this book.

There are checklists, reports, tips and tools to help you grow your current business and ways to find out how to own your very own franchise.

Go Check out our Bonuses at:

www.FranchiseLeadersBook.com